STAMP DECORATING

A step-by-step guidebook and inspirational sourcebook, with over 80 projects and techniques

STEWART AND SALLY WALTON

HH
HERMES HOUSE

This edition is published by Hermes House

Hermes House
is an imprint of
Anness Publishing Ltd
Hermes House
88–89 Blackfriars Road
London SE1 8HA
tel. 020 7401 2077; fax 020 7633 9499
info@anness.com

A CIP catalogue record for this book is available from the British Library.

Publisher: Joanna Lorenz
Editorial Director: Judith Simons
Project Editor: Felicity Forster
Copy Editor: Judy Cox
Photographer: Graham Rae
Stylists: Diana Civil, Andrea Spencer and Fanny Ward
Designer: Ian Sandom
Jacket Design: Adelle Morris
Editorial Reader: Jay Thundercliffe
Production Controller: Steve Lang

Previously published in two separate volumes,
Stamp Magic and *Stamp Decorating*

1 3 5 7 9 10 8 6 4 2

CONTENTS

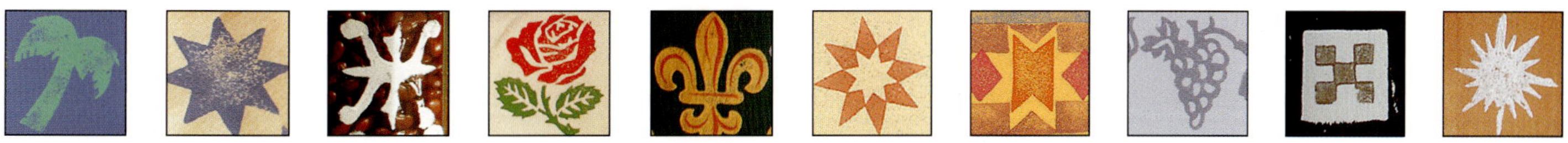

STAMPING BASICS

The stamp decorating idea comes from the rubber office stamp and it uses the same principle – all the equipment you will need is a stamp and some colour. Commercial stamps are readily available, but included in this book is practical advice on how to create your own stamps from wood or sponge, rubber or linoleum – almost any material that will hold colour and release it. Stamps can be used with an ink pad, but a small foam roller gives a better effect: just coat the stamp with ink or ordinary household paint – this makes stamping a fairly inexpensive option. Follow the tips on application techniques and paint effects to achieve the look best suited to your home.

ABOVE: Simple home-made or ready-made stamps, printed at different angles, make a lovely alternative to machine-printed wallpaper.

LEFT: If you have never tried stamping before, begin with a small project such as these book covers, using just one bold stamp.

CREATING STAMPS

There is a huge range of ready-made stamps to choose from, but it is also very satisfying to make your own unique stamps. The following pages show you how to make several kinds of stamp, using different materials. These are often suitable for different surfaces and uses. For example, flexible foam stamps make printing on to a curved glass surface a much easier proposition, and you can also create large shapes. Wood and lino stamps are more difficult to cut, but you may want to graduate to these once you have gained experience and confidence. A good way to begin is with the humble potato-cut. Once you have started creating your own stamps, you won't want to stop!

WOOD AND LINOLEUM STAMPS

Stamped prints were first made with carved wooden blocks. Indian textiles are still produced by hand in this way and it has recently become possible to buy traditional carved printing blocks. Designs are cut in outline and the backgrounds are scooped out to leave the pattern shapes standing proud of the surface. Ink is applied, either by dipping the block or rolling colour on to the surface. The design is stamped and appears in reverse. The craft of making wooden printing blocks takes time to learn: you need special tools that are razor sharp, and an understanding about cutting with or against the grain. Practise on a bonded wood like marine plywood, which is relatively easy to carve.

ABOVE: Create the effect of wood blocks (top) with handmade linocuts (bottom).

Linoleum blocks are available from art and craft suppliers and usually come ready mounted in a range of sizes. Lino is a natural material made from ground cork and linseed oil on a webbed string backing. It is cut in the same way as wood, but has a less resistant texture and no grain to contend with, so is simple to cut.

To make a lino stamp you will need to trace a design and reverse the tracing before transferring it to the lino; this way you will print the design the right way around. Fill in all the background areas with a permanent marker pen: these are the parts to be scooped out, leaving the design proud of the surface. You will need at least three tools – a craft knife, a V-shaped gouge and a scoop. All the tools should be kept as sharp as possible to make cutting easier and safer. Lino is easiest to cut when slightly warm, so place the block on a radiator for ten minutes before cutting. Hold down the block with your spare hand behind your cutting hand, then if the tool slips you will not hurt yourself.

FOAM STAMPS

Different types of foam are characterized by their density. The main types used for stamp-making in this book are: high-density foam, such as upholstery foam; medium-density sponge, such as a kitchen sponge; and low-density sponge, such as a bath sponge. The different densities of foam are each suited to a particular kind of project; on the whole, medium- or low-density sponges are best for bold solid shapes, and high-density foam for fine details. Polystyrene foam (Styrofoam) can also be used but must be mounted on to hardboard. When the glue has dried, the polystyrene can be cut through to the board and the background can be lifted, leaving the design as a stamp.

ABOVE: Home-made stamps cut from high- and medium-density foam.

RUBBER STAMPS

Rubber stamps have come out of the office and playroom and emerged as remarkable interior decorating tools. Shops have sprung up dealing exclusively in an incredible range of stamp designs and the mail-order selections are astounding. The advantage of these pre-cut stamps is that you are instantly ready to transform fabric, furniture, even walls – and there can be no quicker way to add pattern to a surface. However, rubber stamps are most suited to small projects that require fine detail.

There are two methods of creating your own rubber stamp. The first is to design on paper and then have a rubber-stamp company make one for you. This is worth doing if you intend to make good use of the stamp, and not just use it for a small, one-off project. Custom-made stamps are quite expensive to produce, so unless money is no object you may like to consider a second option. You can also make stamps by carving your design into an ordinary eraser. Many erasers are now made of a plastic compound instead of actual rubber, but the surface is smooth and easy to cut into. The best motifs to use on these eraser stamps are small geometric shapes, which can be used to build up patterns or border designs.

To make a sponge stamp, first trace your chosen design then lightly spray the back of the pattern with adhesive, which will make it tacky but removable. Stick the pattern on to the foam and use a sharp craft knife to cut around the shape. Remove any background by cutting across to meet the outlines. If you are using medium- or low-density foam, part it after the initial outline cut, then cut right through to the other side. High-density foam can be cut into and carved out in finer detail. It is also less absorbent, so you get a smoother, less textured print. If you are stamping over a large area, you will find the stamp easier to use if you mount the foam on to a hardboard base and use wood glue to attach a small wooden door knob to the back. This will then act as a convenient handle for you to hold.

RIGHT: Commercial rubber stamps are available in designs to suit all tastes.

JACOBEAN POLYSTYRENE FLOWER

Polystyrene (Styrofoam) is easy to cut and gives good, clean edges. Always mount the polystyrene on to a piece of hardboard backing before you begin to draw and cut your design. When the glue has dried the polystyrene can be cut through to the board, leaving the design as a stamp.

You will need

- sheet of polystyrene foam (Styrofoam), approximately 1cm/½in thick
- piece of hardboard, the same size as the polystyrene
- wood glue or PVA (white) glue
- felt-tipped pen
- craft knife

1 Stick the sheet of polystyrene (Styrofoam) and hardboard backing together with wood glue or PVA (white) glue.

2 Without waiting for the glue to set, draw the design using a felt-tipped pen. Remember that the pattern will reverse when printed.

3 Cut around the outline of the design using a craft knife. If this is done before the glue has set, these pieces will pull away easily.

4 Cut the edging details, removing unwanted pieces of polystyrene as you go.

5 Make shallow, angular cuts to scoop out the pattern details of the flower design. Use a new craft knife blade for this so that the cuts are sharp and you do not accidentally lift adjoining particles of polystyrene that have been only partially separated.

GEOMETRIC BORDER DESIGN

This border stamp is made from high-density foam. A good quality upholstery foam is recommended. The piece used here was sold by a camping supply store for use as a portable, compact mattress. The high-density foam is not very absorbent so creates a smoother, less textured print.

You will need

- wood glue or PVA (white) glue
- high-density foam, such as upholstery foam, cut to the size of your design
- hardboard, cut to the same size
- felt-tipped pen
- ruler
- craft knife
- wooden block, for the handle

1 Stick the foam on to the hardboard by applying wood glue or PVA (white) glue to the rough side.

2 Without waiting for the glue to set, draw a geometric pattern on to the foam using a felt-tipped pen and ruler. Use a craft knife to outline the sections to be cut away, then lift them out. If the glue is still tacky, this will be much easier to do.

3 Finally, using wood glue or PVA glue, stick the wooden block in the middle of the stamp back, to act as a handle. Allow to dry thoroughly.

SQUIGGLE FOAM STAMP

Foam comes in all shapes, sizes and densities. Make a visit to a specialist foam dealer, as inspiration for new ideas often springs from the discovery of new materials. Here is an idea for making a bold stamp in an original way which does not require any drawing or cutting.

You will need

- masking tape
- length of cylindrical foam, about 2cm/¾in diameter
- wood glue or PVA (white) glue
- hardboard

1 Lay out a length of masking tape, sticky side up. Twist the foam into a squiggle shape, pressing it on to the middle section of the tape.

2 Apply wood glue or PVA (white) glue to the untaped side of the foam and turn it face-down on to the hardboard. Fold the tape ends under the hardboard to hold the foam in place while the glue sets. When the glue is dry, peel off the masking tape.

FLORAL LINOCUT

Cutting linoleum is a simple technique to master. Linoleum blocks are available in a range of sizes from art and craft suppliers. You will be delighted with the intricacy of the motifs you can create using this medium. Remember to warm your linoleum ten mintues before cutting.

You will need

- tracing paper
- pencil
- sheet of carbon paper
- linoleum block
- masking tape
- craft knife
- lino-cutting tools: a V-shaped gouge and a U-shaped scoop

1 Make a tracing of your chosen motif, the same size as the linoleum block. Slip a sheet of carbon paper (chalky side down) between the tracing and the linoleum, then tape the edges with masking tape.

2 Draw over the lines of the motif with a sharp pencil. The tracing will appear on the linoleum block.

3 Remove the paper and cut around the outline with a craft knife. Cut any fine detail or straight lines by making shallow, angular cuts from each side, then scoop out the V-shaped sections.

4 Cut out the rest of the pattern using the lino tools – the U-shaped scoop for removing large areas of background, and the V-shaped gouge for cutting the finer curves and pattern details. Hold the lino down firmly, with your spare hand placed behind your cutting hand to avoid accidents.

POTATO PRINT SUNBURST

Most of us learn the technique of using potatoes for printing as very young schoolchildren. Potato prints are quick and simple to do but look amazingly effective, and they are an inexpensive way to achieve bright, bold results. This enjoyable technique should not be overlooked by adults.

You will need

- medium-sized raw potato
- sharp kitchen knife
- fine felt-tipped pen
- craft knife

1 Use a sharp kitchen knife to make a single cut right through the potato. This will give you a smooth surface to work with.

2 Draw the sunburst motif on to the potato with a fine felt-tipped pen. Remember that motifs reverse when stamped, although with the sunburst motif used here it will make no difference.

3 Use a craft knife to cut the outline, then under-cut and scoop out the background. Potato stamps will not last longer than a few hours before they deteriorate, so keep a tracing of your motif if your project cannot be completed in one go. The design can then be re-cut using a fresh potato.

APPLICATION TECHNIQUES

In the world of stamping, the coating of a stamp with colour is always known as inking, regardless of the substance applied. There are no hard and fast rules about what can or cannot be used – any substance that coats a stamp and is then released on to a surface when stamped, will be suitable. Stamp inkpads are available from art and craft suppliers or specialist stamp stores, and come in a wide range of shapes, sizes and colours. Some contain permanent ink and others are water-based and washable. Paints can be applied with brushes or rollers, or spread on to a flat surface and the stamp dipped into them. Experiment with different paints and inks and always test the stamp on scrap paper first before starting a project.

Using a brush

This is a way of applying thick water-based paint such as emulsion (latex) or artist's acrylic. One big advantage here is that you can use several colours on one stamp in a very controlled way. This would not be possible if you were inverting the stamp on to an inkpad.

Using a roller

Place a blob of paint on one side of a flat plate and run a small rubber roller through it several times until it is covered evenly with colour. Run the roller over the rubber stamp to transfer the paint. Make a test print on scrap paper first, as this method sometimes overloads the stamp with paint.

Using an inkpad

Simply press the rubber stamp lightly on to the surface of the stamp inkpad. Check that the stamp is evenly coated, then make your print. It is difficult to overload the stamp using this method.

Using a sponge

Spread an even coating of paint on to a flat plate and simply dip the sponge stamp into it. Check that the stamp is evenly coated, then make a test print on scrap paper to gauge the effect. Sponge is more absorbent than rubber, so you will need to use more paint.

Using miniature inkpads

These small inkpads come in a range of brilliant colours and metallics. Just wipe them across the rubber stamp. As with brush application you can use more than one colour at a time, but take care to avoid colours mixing on the stamp pads.

Using a glaze

You can apply a translucent colour glaze using a stamp or potato cut. Make up some wallpaper paste and tint it with liquid watercolour paint or water-based ink. Dip the stamp in the mixture and print. The paste dries to a clear sheen with a hint of colour.

PAINT EFFECTS

The same rubber stamp can be made to have several different characteristics, depending on the colours and inks that you choose. The sun stamp below illustrates this very well. It has been used to create cool and warm effects, using a glittering glaze and brush-applied paints.

Metallic print

This metallic print was made with equal parts PVA (white) glue and water, to half of metallic powder. This mixture was applied to the stamp with a rubber roller. When dry, the glittering powder is held in a transparent glaze.

Two-colour print

The same sun stamp was coated with two different coloured paints, applied with a brush. When paint is applied in this way, it is possible to separate areas of colour, which is impossible when using an inkpad.

Light effects

This effect uses the almost powdery appearance of a medium-density sponge stamp lightly applied to a colourwashed wall. Emulsion (latex) paint was mixed half and half with prepared wallpaper paste, which gives a gelatinous quality when wet and a transparent glaze once dry.

OVERPRINTING EFFECTS

Once you have cut a complicated design like the one below, you can experiment with building up the pattern by adding colour and overprinting. This design can be printed one way, then turned around to print in the other direction. The second print fills in the triangle shapes that were left blank. This works particularly well for the central pattern. Care must be taken not to re-ink the border lines, because they are less effective when printed with more than one colour.

1 The first print was made in light yellow emulsion (latex) paint on to a light blue colourwashed wall.

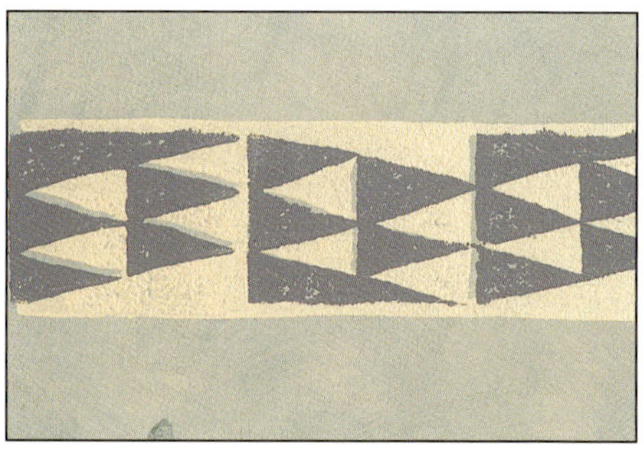

2 The stamp was cleaned and re-inked with dark blue-grey paint, avoiding the thin border. The print was made with the stamp turned around to face the other direction, but lined up to fit exactly on top of the first print.

3 Other colours were applied to selected areas of the stamp, including a separate colour for each of the border lines.

SPECIAL-EFFECT PAINT MIXTURES

There are many different kinds of paint available these days and they are often sold in huge self-service warehouses. Sometimes it is impossible to find any specialist assistance for your particular project. In this book we have tried to narrow down the paint options by suggesting either acrylic artist's colour, watercolour (available in small jars as a ready-mixed liquid from art and craft suppliers) or emulsion (latex) paint. This should not mean, however, that all paint finishes look the same; there are a number of very simple ways to vary the intensity and texture of these paints, using wallpaper paste or PVA (white) glue. The step-by-step photographs below explain the different methods and effects that can be achieved.

WATERCOLOUR PAINT AND WALLPAPER PASTE

This mixture is only suitable for surfaces that do not need wiping clean, so use it for paper and card but not for walls.

You will need

- wallpaper paste and water
- plate
- paintbrush
- ready-mixed liquid watercolour paint
- scrap paper

1 Mix the wallpaper paste to a slightly thinner consistency than usual. It will thicken after five minutes, when you will be able to thin it by adding more water. It should have a sloppy consistency.

2 Add a drop of ready-mixed liquid watercolour paint. The colour is intense and a small amount goes a long way. Add and stir in as many more drops as you need, testing the paint on a sheet of scrap paper to judge the brightness. The wallpaper paste gives the mixture the thickness that is needed for stamping – watercolour paint on its own would not be suitable.

EMULSION PAINT AND WALLPAPER PASTE

This mixture adds another dimension to the usual texture of emulsion (latex) paint. It is suitable for all household decorating, and the wallpaper paste makes it particularly suited to sponge stamping. The advantage of this mixture is that it is washable when dry, so it is suitable for all household decorating work. When dry, the wallpaper paste is transparent and adds an attractive glazed texture to the emulsion paint. Its gelatinous quality works well with sponge stamps.

You will need

- wallpaper paste and water
- plate
- paintbrush
- emulsion (latex) paint
- small wooden block
- foam stamp
- bowl of water
- kitchen paper
- scrap paper

1 Mix the wallpaper paste with the required amount of water according to the manufacturer's instructions. Make a glaze using one part emulsion (latex) paint to two parts wallpaper paste. Mix together well.

2 When you have achieved the desired colour and consistency, prop up one side of the plate with a small wooden block, or something similar. The plate should feel stable and remain in this position to provide an even coating of paint for stamping.

3 Soak the foam stamp in a bowl of water. All foam works a lot better for stamping if it is damp rather than dry as it will absorb and release the paint mixture more readily. Lift the stamp out of the water and squeeze out the excess moisture into a sheet of kitchen paper.

4 Scoop up some of the paint and use it to coat the raised side of the plate with a thin layer of colour. Dip the foam stamp into this.

5 First, make a test print on to a sheet of scrap paper to ensure that the stamp is not overloaded with paint. This photograph shows the effect of the final fish stamp printed on a light blue colourwashed background.

SURFACE FINISHES

When you print with stamps, the shape of the design remains constant but there are many different finishes that can be achieved. The factors affecting these are the surface that you stamp on to as well as the material used to make up the stamp, and the substance that you stamp with. All of these can vary enormously. To illustrate some of the possible effects that you can achieve, we have printed motifs with emulsion (latex) paint and then experimented with simple different finishes.

ALTERING EFFECTS

Once the pattern has been stamped on the wall (or on a wooden surface), there are various ways that you can alter its regular appearance. You can make the original print appear softer or darker using the following simple techniques. All you need is some abrasive paper (sandpaper) or tinted varnish.

1 This is the basic design. A foam rubber stamp was pressed into blue emulsion (latex) paint and printed on an emulsion-painted wall.

2 The print was allowed to dry and then it was lightly rubbed back using fine-grade abrasive paper (sandpaper).

3 This stamp has been darkened with a coat of tinted antiquing varnish. As well as protecting the surface, it deepens the colour and adds a slight sheen.

DEPTH EFFECTS

Varnish can be used over your designs to add depth to the colour and protect the wall surface. These prints, made with a polystyrene (Styrofoam) stamp, demonstrate the changes made by coats of varnish. Tinted varnish comes in many shades, and enriches the colour with each application.

1 This is the basic stamped pattern in grey emulsion (latex) paint on a light buttermilk-coloured background.

2 This is the surface after one coat of tinted varnish was applied. It has deepened the yellow considerably.

3 A second coat of the same varnish was applied and the colour has turned deep pine-yellow.

WOOD APPLICATION

You can use most types of paint on wood, although some will need sealing with a protective coat of varnish. New wood needs to be sealed with a coat of shellac – this stops resin leaking through the grain. Below are some examples of rubber, sponge and potato prints made on wood with a variety of media. Woodstains, varnishes and paints have different properties and create different effects depending on the stamp used. The wood grain gives extra texture and interest to the stamped design.

This example shows emulsion paint applied with a rubber stamp.

This print was made with emulsion paint applied with a sponge stamp.

This is an example of emulsion (latex) paint applied with a potato-cut.

This shows an example of woodstain applied with a rubber stamp.

This print was made with woodstain applied with a sponge stamp.

This is the effect of woodstain applied with a potato-cut.

This is an example of tinted varnish applied with a rubber stamp.

This print was made with tinted varnish applied with a potato-cut.

This shows an example of red ink applied with a potato-cut.

FABRIC APPLICATION

There are several types of fabric ink suitable for stamp printing – the two main types are those used to stamp directly on to fabric and those which are stamped on to paper first and then heat-transferred. The inks used in these samples are all stamped directly, but you can see transfer printing in the Trailblazer Scarf project in this book. Although the prints shown below have all been made with fabric printing ink, different methods of application have been used. Some stamps are more successful than others, but all produce their own distinctive effects. Experiment with different fabrics and inks from the wide range available, and see the colour transformation take place.

This multi-coloured print was made by inking a high-density foam stamp in two different colours.

These prints were made with wine bottle corks with bored holes. Corks make very effective stamps.

This print shows an example of a fish made by inking a high-density foam stamp in a single colour.

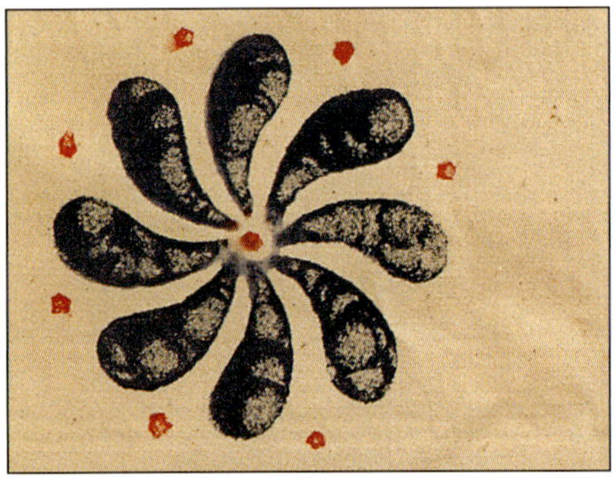

This high-density foam stamp was inked in blue with a halo of red dots.

This fleur-de-lys print was made with a high-density foam stamp and red fabric ink for a crisp, intense finish.

These red and blue potato-cut circles were inked with two colours to create an irregular pattern.

This print is an example made with a ready-made rubber stamp.

This print effect was made by using a sponge stamp.

This shows an example of a print made with a potato-cut.

CERAMIC AND GLASS APPLICATION

Different surfaces bring out the different qualities of paint. The kind of stamp used will also have a big influence on the final result. To illustrate the different effects that can be achieved, we have used motifs cut from rubber, foam and potato, with a variety of inks, paints and stains. Some choices may seem unusual, like woodstain on terracotta, but experimentation can produce unexpected successes!

The print on this flowerpot was made with emulsion (latex) paint using a sponge.

This print was made with woodstain applied with a sponge.

The print on this pot was made with tinted varnish using a rubber stamp.

This shows a print made with emulsion paint applied with a rubber stamp.

This print was made with woodstain applied with a potato-cut.

This is an example of a print made with tinted varnish applied with a potato-cut.

These prints were made on a ceramic plate with acrylic enamel paint, applied with a potato-cut (top left), a sponge (top right), and a rubber stamp (bottom).

These glass prints were made with acrylic enamel paint thinned with clear acrylic varnish, using a sponge (top left), rubber stamp (top right) and potato-cut (bottom).

These prints were applied to glass with a coil of foam dipped into emulsion paint. The emulsion was left to dry, then covered with a protective coat of clear varnish.

TILE APPLICATION

These are just a small selection of the different effects that can be achieved by stamp printing on to tiles. Remember to clean the tiles thoroughly before decorating. We recommend that you always use acrylic enamel paints and, wherever possible, decorate them before you put them on a wall because this gives you the chance to add to their resilience by baking them in the oven. Always follow the manufacturer's instructions for times and temperatures, and ensure your tiles can withstand this treatment. You can create borders, overall patterns or individual highlights.

These little circles were made by dipping bored wine bottle corks into red and blue paint, and printing in rows.

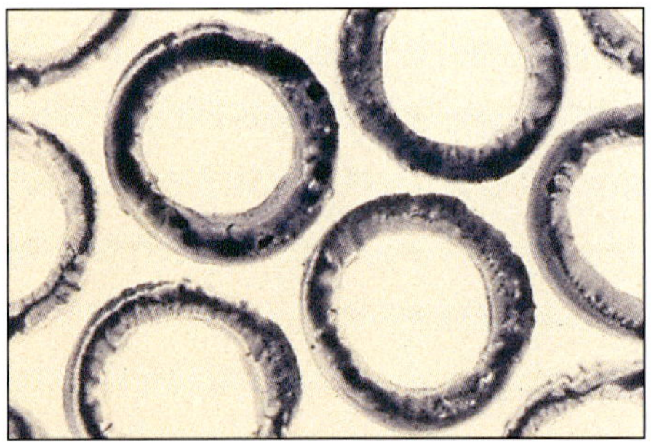

These larger circles were made using a potato-cut. The transparent effect comes from the potato starch mixing in with the paint.

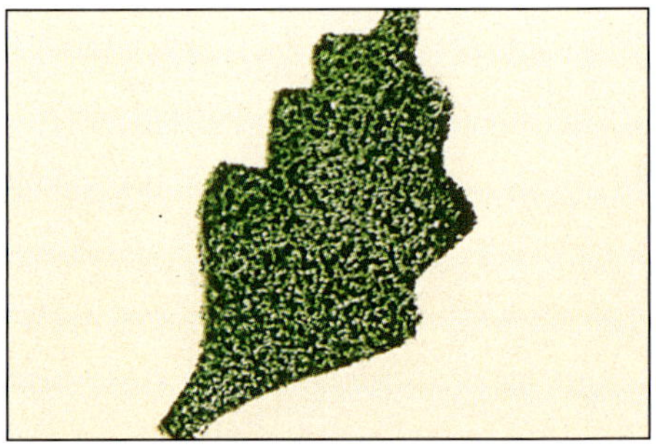

This print shows an example made with a shaped, medium-density sponge. The textured effect is due to the density of the sponge.

This pattern was made using small rubber stamps cut from an eraser. A zigzag pattern like this makes a good border.

This heart was cut from medium-density sponge. The textured effect is opaque but "powdery".

This pattern was made by dipping straight strips of high-density foam into red and blue paint. The thickness of the strips can be varied to produce a tartan pattern.

A small square of foam was used to print this chequerboard effect. This pattern is quite time-consuming, but very effective.

This high-density foam stamp was coloured with a brush to make a three-colour print. These make good highlights mixed in with single-colour prints.

This border was made with a medium-density foam block, printed in different colours. The edges must be aligned accurately for best effect.

DESIGNING WITH STAMPS

To design the pattern of your stamps, you need to find a compromise between printing totally at random and measuring precisely to achieve a machine-printed regularity. To do this, you can use the stamp block itself to give you a means of measuring your pattern, or try strips of paper, squares of card or a length of string to act as a plumbline. Experiment by using a stamp pad on scrap paper to plan your design but always wash and dry the stamp before proceeding to print the main event.

Using paper cut-outs

The easiest way to plan your design is to stamp as many pattern elements as you need on to scrap paper. Cut them out with scissors and use them to arrange the position of your finished stamped prints.

Creating a repeat pattern

Use a strip of paper as a measuring device for repeat patterns. Cut the strip the length of one row of the pattern. Use the stamp block to mark where each print will go, with equal spaces in between. You could mark up a vertical strip, too. Position the horizontal strip against this as you print.

Using a paper spacing device

This method is very simple. Decide on the distance between prints and cut a strip of paper to that size. Each time you stamp, place the strip against the edge of the previous print and line up the edge of the block with the other side of the strip. Use a longer strip to measure the distance required.

Creating an irregular pattern

If your design doesn't fit into a regular grid, plan the pattern first on paper. Cut out paper shapes to represent the spaces and use these to position the finished pattern. Alternatively, raise a motif above the previous one by stamping above a strip of card positioned on the baseline.

Devising a larger design

Use the stamps in groups to make up a larger design. Try stamping four together in a block, or partially overlapping an edge so that only a section of the stamp is shown. Use the stamps upside down, back to back and rotated in different ways. Experiment on scrap paper first.

Using a plumbline

Attach a plumbline at ceiling height to hang down the wall. Hold a card (stock) square behind the plumbline so that the string cuts through two opposite corners. Mark all four points, then move the card square down. Continue in this way to make a grid for stamping a regular pattern.

WALLS AND SURFACES

Decorating walls and surfaces should not be a high-anxiety activity; it should be enjoyable to do and rewarding to view. Stamping is not only both of these, but also the quickest and easiest way to put a pattern on a wall. There are many different looks that you can achieve with stamps, depending upon the materials you use. Pre-cut rubber stamps produce a fine, sophisticated and subtle effect, while home-made foam stamps are often simple and bold. Both kinds of stamp give varying results according to how much pressure you use: regular pressure produces identical motifs; irregular pressure produces a more hand-painted look.

ABOVE: A single stamp, applied using varying amounts of paint, gives an exclusive hand-blocked effect.

LEFT: Like all stamping, the materials required are very simple. The string, with a weight attached, serves as a plumbline.

TUSCAN FRIEZE

Three stamps are used in this project to transform a dull space into a wall frieze that you will want to preserve forever. The finished wall will bring a touch of Tuscany into your home, even when the sky is a gloomy grey outside. The wall is divided at dado height with a strong burgundy red below and a warm cream above to visually lower the ceiling. The vine leaf pattern has been stamped on to a grid of pencil marks that is simple to measure out using a square of card (stock) and a plumbline. The lines are hand-painted using a wooden batten (furring strip) as a hand rest but you could also stick parallel strips of masking tape around the walls and fill in the stripes between.

You will need

- tape measure
- pencil
- ruler
- emulsion (latex) paint in cream, burgundy, terracotta, white and black
- large household paintbrush
- wallpaper paste, mixed according to the manufacturer's instructions
- plate
- foam roller
- grape, tendril and leaf stamps
- thin strip of card (stock)
- long-bristled lining brush
- straight-edged wooden batten (furring strip), 1m/1yd long
- plumbline
- card, 15 x 15cm/6 x 6in
- square-tipped artist's paintbrush
- clear gloss, matt (flat) or satin varnish and brush

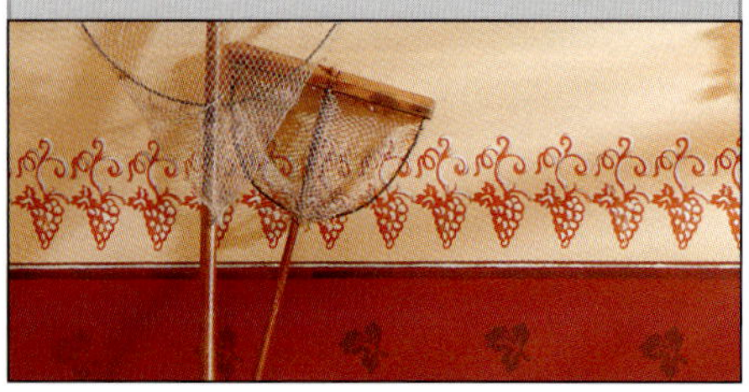

1 Measure the height of a dado (chair) rail and draw a line around the wall with a ruler and pencil. Paint the wall above the line cream and the area below burgundy. Mix roughly equal amounts of wallpaper paste, burgundy and terracotta paint on a plate.

2 Run the roller through the mixture until it is evenly coated and ink the grape stamp. Align the strip of card (stock) with the top of the burgundy section. Rest the base of the stamp block on the card to stamp a row of grapes.

3 Ink the tendril stamp and stamp a tendril at the top of each bunch of grapes. Allow some of the prints to be paler than others as the paint wears off the stamp block, to give a deliberately faded and patchy effect.

4 Mix a little cream paint into some white. With the lining brush, apply highlights to the grapes and the tendrils. Let the brushstrokes vary in direction and weight to add to the hand-painted look. Support your painting hand with your free hand.

5 Hold the batten (furring strip) just below the top edge of the burgundy section and rest your painting hand on it. Slide your hand along the batten to paint a smooth, thin line in off-white. Practise this movement first and try to relax your hand to avoid jerky lines. A slight waviness to the line will not spoil the effect. Try to avoid having to paint over the line, as a single, fresh brushstroke looks better.

6 Attach a plumbline above dado height, just in from one corner and so that it hangs down to the skirting (base) board. Place the card square against the wall so that the string cuts through the top and bottom corners. Mark all the corner points in pencil.

7 Move the card down so that the top corner rests on the lowest pencil mark. Complete one column of the grid in this way, then move the plumbline across and continue until the lower wall is completely covered with a grid of pencil marks.

8 Mix a small amount of black paint into the burgundy to deepen the colour. Spread some dark burgundy paint on to a plate and run the roller through it until it is evenly coated. Ink the leaf stamp and make a print on one of the pencil marks.

9 Position the stamp just above or just below the pencil mark each time to create a regular pattern over the whole lower wall.

10 Move the batten about 2.5cm/1in from the cream dado line and use the square-tipped artist's paintbrush to paint a second, broader line. Keep the line as fresh as possible; visible brushstrokes are preferable to solid, flat colour. Apply a coat of varnish to the lower wall to seal and protect the paint.

RIGHT: The grape motifs are printed with two stamps, one for the grapes and one for the tendrils. These are then highlighted by hand using a lining brush to create a hand-painted look. This technique can be applied to give extra depth and interest to other stamped designs.

FLORAL SPRIG

This all-over country floral motif is made with three sponge stamps. The background colour is creamy yellow and the sprigs echo the colours used on and below the dado (chair) rail. The sprigs change direction with every alternate print, giving the pattern its dynamic energy. Vary the intensity of the colour by applying less pressure on some prints, as well as making several prints before recharging your sponge. The most time-consuming part of the project will be marking out a grid of pencil marks across the whole wall surface, but once that is in place the stamped pattern will grow very quickly. This pattern will suit a large or small room equally well.

You will need

- tracing paper
- pencil
- spray adhesive
- low-density sponge, such as a bath sponge
- felt-tipped pen
- craft knife
- plumbline
- card (stock), 14 x 14cm/5½ x 5½in
- emulsion (latex) paint in brick-red and dusky blue
- plates

1 Trace, transfer and cut out the pattern shapes from the template section. Lightly spray the shapes with adhesive and place on the sponge. Use a craft knife to cut out the shapes.

2 Attach a plumbline at ceiling height to drop down to dado (chair) rail height. Place the card (stock) square on the diagonal, with the plumbline running through the centre. Mark all the corners on the wall in pencil. Move the square up and continue to use this system to mark a grid on the wall.

3 Spread the brick-red and dusky blue paint on to separate plates. Make the first print on to scrap paper to make sure that the stamp is not overloaded. Using the pencil marks as your guide, stamp blue stem shapes. Change the direction of the curve from left to right with each alternate print.

4 Use the same blue paint to stamp the leaf shape on to the base of each stem, alternating the direction of each print as you did with the stem.

5 Dip the flower-shaped sponge into the brick-red paint. Make an initial print on scrap paper to make sure the stamp is not overloaded. Stamp the flower shapes on to the tops of the stems. Vary the pressure used, to give different densities of colour.

ABOVE: Home-made sponge stamps, using low-density sponge such as a bath sponge, give a delicate, soft effect. This lovely design is an ideal example of how changing the direction of the prints brings vitality and energy – the flowers really look as if they are moving in the breeze.

SPINNING SUN MOTIF

This rich combination of spicy red-brown and earthy yellow seems to infuse the room with warmth and the spinning sun motif has a timeless quality. The pattern is a lot of fun to paint, because once you've marked out the grid it grows very quickly, and using a single colour makes for very easy stamping. Colourwash the wall with yellow-ochre emulsion (latex) paint, diluted half and half with water. Use random brushstrokes, working within arm's reach. The finish should look patchy rather than even – like dappled sunlight. Paint the lower section a deep terracotta.

You will need

- tape measure
- spirit level
- pencil
- paintbrush
- emulsion (latex) paint in terracotta and yellow-ochre
- clear satin varnish
- tracing paper
- craft knife
- adhesive spray
- high-density foam rubber, such as upholstery foam
- plate
- plumbline
- card (stock), 15 x 13cm/6 x 5in

1 Divide the wall at dado (chair) rail height, using a tape measure, spirit level and pencil. Paint terracotta below the line and yellow-ochre above. Apply a coat of clear satin varnish to the terracotta. Trace, transfer and cut out the pattern shapes from the template section. Lightly spray with adhesive and place them on the foam rubber. Cut around the designs with a craft knife.

2 Spread an even coating of terracotta paint on to a plate and press the smaller stamp into it. Make a test print on scrap paper to make sure that the stamp is not overloaded with paint, then stamp a row above the dado rail height. Attach a plumbline at ceiling height, and mark out a grid using the card (stock) and a pencil, as described in the Sunstar Wall project.

3 Press the larger stamp into the terracotta paint and test print on scrap paper. Following the grid of pencil marks, stamp the large sunwheels on to the wall.

4 Connect the sunwheels by stamping three small sunstars in a straight line between them, across the whole surface of the wall.

RIGHT: Use a plumbline such as a weighted piece of string to measure complex grid designs accurately.

SUNSTAR WALL

It is hard to believe that decorating can be this easy. Gone are the days of the perfectly even finish of flat colour – now we are more attuned to the comfort of patchy paintwork. If you have a minute and a piece of sponge to spare, that is all it takes to make the sunstar stamp. It could not be simpler. The wall was colourwashed with diluted coffee-coloured emulsion (latex) paint. Just mix the paint half and half with water, stir well and paint the wall using random sweeping strokes. Work within an arm's reach and blend any hard edges with a dryish brush before the paint dries.

You will need

- medium-density sponge, such as a kitchen sponge
- felt-tipped pen
- craft knife
- plumbline
- card (stock), 26 x 26cm/10 x 10in
- pencil
- wallpaper paste, for mixing
- cup
- plate
- emulsion (latex) paint in terracotta
- paintbrush

1 Draw a circle on the sponge using a felt-tipped pen and a round object as a template.

2 Draw the shape of the sunstar within the circle, referring to the pattern in the template section. The motif can be made to any size.

3 Cut out the circle with a craft knife. Cut around the shape, then part the sponge and cut all the way through.

4 Cut around the drawn pattern shape and discard the sponge scraps.

5 Attach a plumbline at ceiling height (this can be done with masking tape). Place the card (stock) square on the diagonal behind the line, so that it falls through two points. Mark all the corners on the wall in pencil, then move the square up, continuing to mark all the corners. Use this system, moving the line along the wall, until a grid of pencil marks covers the wall.

6 Mix a cup of wallpaper paste, place a blob on the plate alongside an equal amount of terracotta paint and blend the two together with a paintbrush. Press the sponge into the mixture and make a test print on a sheet of scrap paper. Then start stamping the wall, using the pencil marks as your guide. Mix the paste and paint together as you go, so that the density of the colour varies.

7 Continue stamping so that the sunstars form a regular pattern across the whole wall.

MEXICAN BORDER

Banish gloomy weather with vibrant sunshine-yellow and intense sky-blue. With the heat turned up, it will be time to add an ethnic touch by stamping an Aztec border along the walls. Use the patterns from the template section to cut basic geometric shapes from a medium-density sponge, like the ones used for washing dishes. Mix shades of green with purples, add an earthy red and then stamp on diamonds of fuschia-pink for its sheer brilliance. It's a bold statement. These days emulsion (latex) paint is available in a huge range of exciting colours. Try not to be tempted by muted colours for this border – it will lose much of its impact. Bright colours go well with natural materials, like straw hats, sisal matting, wicker baskets and clay pots.

You will need

- tape measure
- spirit level
- pencil
- emulsion (latex) paint in sunshine-yellow and deep sky-blue
- paint rollers and tray
- small amounts of emulsion paint in light blue-grey, purple, brick-red, fuschia-pink and dark green
- plates
- foam rubber strip
- medium-density sponge, such as a kitchen sponge, cut into the pattern shapes from the template section

1 Divide the wall at dado (chair) rail height using a tape measure, spirit level and pencil. Paint the upper part sunshine-yellow and the lower part deep sky-blue using the paint rollers. Then use the spirit level and pencil to draw a parallel line about 15cm/6in above the blue section.

2 Use a foam rubber strip to stamp a light blue-grey line directly above the blue section. Then use the same strip to stamp the top line of the border along the pencil line.

3 Spread an even coating of each of the frieze colours on to separate plates. Use the rectangular and triangular shapes alternately to print a purple row above the bottom line and below the top line. Stamp on to scrap paper first to make sure the stamp is not overloaded.

4 Stamp the largest shape in brick-red, lining it up to fit between the points of the top and bottom triangles. There should be approximately 1cm/½in of background colour showing between this brick-red shape and the triangles.

5 Stamp the diamond shapes in fuschia-pink between the central brick-red motifs. The points of the diamonds should touch the purple rectangular shapes.

6 Finally add a zigzagged edge by overprinting dark green triangles along the light blue-grey lines.

BELOW: Bold geometric shapes and a vibrant mix of colours would transform a landing or a small space such as a dark hallway or a spare bedroom.

SCANDINAVIAN LIVING ROOM

Create a cool atmosphere with this sophisticated Gustavian-influenced wall stamping. This project is less instant than others featured in the book, but the elegance of the result justifies all the preparatory work. The stamps are cut from high-density foam rubber which is mounted on to blocks of composition board, and a small door knob is added for easy handling. Before any stamping can be done, a grid must be drawn across the wall using a plumbline and a card (stock) square. If you find the effect of the two blues too cool, you can add warmth by applying a coat of tinted varnish to the whole wall, including the woodwork. It has the effect of bathing the room in golden sunlight.

You will need

- wood glue or PVA (white) glue
- 2 pieces composition board, 8.5 x 8.5cm/ $3^1/_2$ x $3^1/_2$in
- 2 pieces high-density foam rubber, such as upholstery foam, 8.5 x 8.5cm/ $3^1/_2$ x $3^1/_2$in
- tracing paper
- pencil
- spray adhesive
- craft knife
- ruler
- 2 small wooden door knobs
- plumbline
- card (stock), 18 x 18cm/7 x 7in
- plate
- emulsion (latex) paint in dark blue

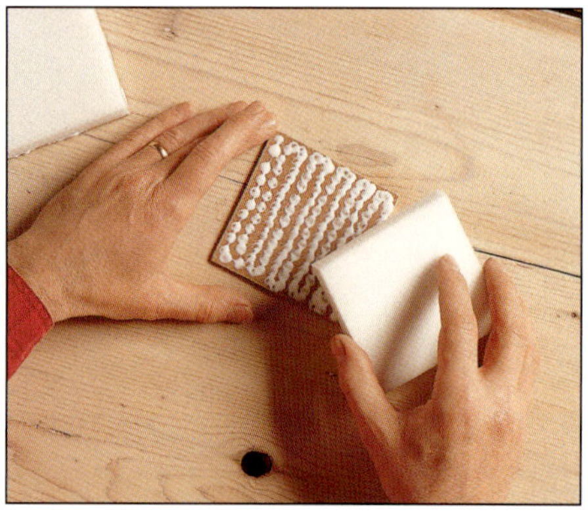

1 Apply glue to the composition board squares and stick the foam rubber on to them. Leave the glue to dry.

2 Trace and transfer the pattern shapes from the template section. Lightly spray with adhesive and place on the foam rubber blocks.

3 Cut around the edges of the designs and remove the paper pattern. Scoop out the background to leave the stamps free of the composition board.

4 Draw two intersecting lines across the back of each square of composition board and glue a wooden door knob in the centre to act as a handle.

5 Attach a plumbline at ceiling height to give a vertical guideline (this can be done with a piece of masking tape). Mark a point 8cm/3¼in above the dado (chair) rail and place one corner of the card (stock) square on it, lined up along the plumbline. Mark all the corners on the wall in pencil, then move the square up, continuing to mark the corners. Use this system to mark a grid of squares across the whole upper wall.

6 One of the stamps has a static motif and the other has a swirl. Use the static one first, dipping it into a plate coated with paint and making the first print on a sheet of scrap paper to make sure that the stamp is not overloaded. Then print up the wall, starting from the 8cm/3¼in mark.

7 Continue printing up the wall, working up the diagonal and following the grid of pencil marks.

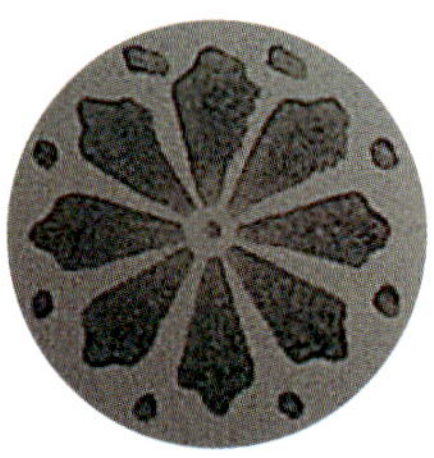

8 Change to the swirl motif, and stamp this pattern in the spaces between the static motifs.

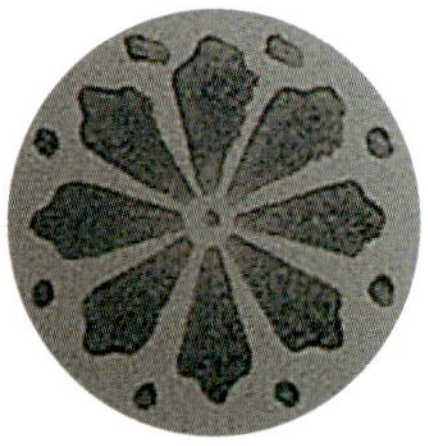

RIGHT: Traditional Scandinavian design has a timeless appeal. Blue and white is the classic combination, and always looks cool and serene. If you prefer, you can stamp the prints in a lighter shade of blue on a plain white wall. Continue the theme with white-painted furniture and simple checked fabrics.

TULIPS AND LEAVES

Corridors, entrance halls and landings are good for "sudden inspiration" decorating jobs, as there is very little furniture to be moved. Make the most of these spaces using warm colours and all-over patterns. Here the woodwork, table and chair are all painted a pale duck-egg blue, which is also used to stamp the leaf pattern on the semi-transparent blind. You can use fabric paint on the blind but it is not absolutely essential, as the blind is unlikely to be washed. A painted border in the same colour as the tulips adds a very smart finishing touch to the walls and small decorative objects such as the wall sconce can be stamped in similar shades.

You will need

- emulsion (latex) paint in terracotta, deep plum and grey-green
- large and small household paintbrushes
- plumbline
- card (stock), 25 x 25cm/10 x 10in
- pencil
- plates
- foam rollers
- tulip and leaf stamps
- ruler
- masking tape (optional)
- scrap paper
- black stamp pad
- scissors
- white, semi-transparent roller blind
- newspaper
- duck-egg blue emulsion paint or fabric paint
- iron (optional)

1 Paint the walls with terracotta emulsion (latex) paint and leave to dry. Attach the plumbline at ceiling height. Hold the card (stock) square against the wall so that the plumbline string cuts through the top and bottom corners of the square. Mark all four points in pencil. Continue moving the square and marking the points to form a grid all over the wall.

2 Spread some deep plum emulsion (latex) paint on to a plate and run a roller through it until it is evenly coated. Ink the tulip stamp and, holding it on the diagonal, make a print on each pencil mark. Position the stamp just above or just below the mark each time to create a regular pattern.

3 Change the angle of the stamp from right to left with each alternate print to give the pattern a hand-printed rather than a machine-printed look. Continue stamping tulips until the whole wall is covered.

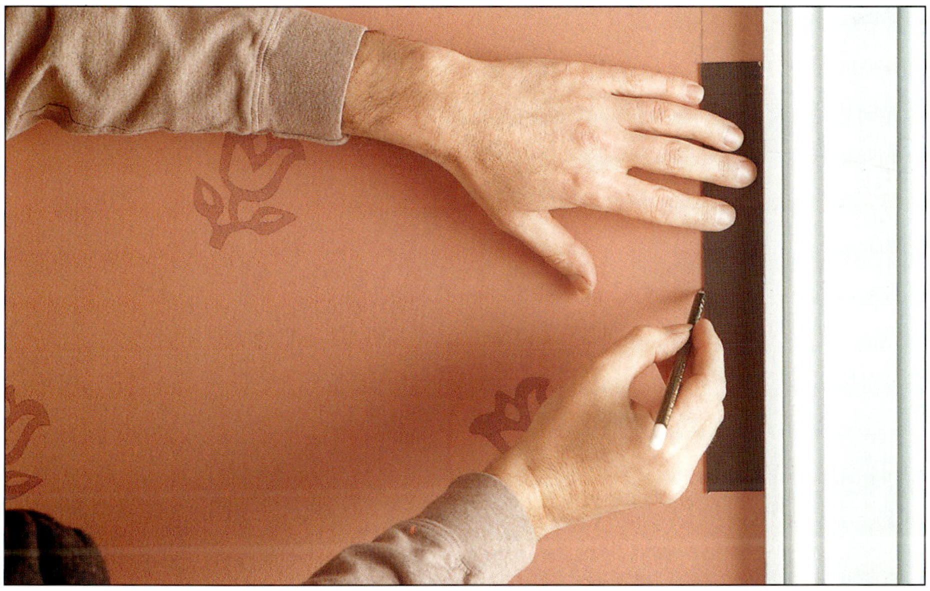

4 Draw a line around the window a ruler's width away from the edge of the window frame. Stick masking tape along the line if you are not confident about painting a straight line.

5 Using the small paintbrush, paint a deep plum border between the edge of the window frame and the pencil line.

6 For the blind, use the stamp pad to print 16 leaves on scrap paper. Alternate two different stamps so that the leaves point in different directions. Cut out the patterns. Lay the blind on newspaper and arrange the leaves to plan the design, starting at the bottom edge.

7 Spread some duck-egg blue emulsion or fabric paint on to a plate and run a roller through it until it is evenly coated. Ink the stamp and remove one paper shape at a time to stamp a leaf in its place.

8 As you complete each row, move the paper patterns up to make the next row, keeping the spacing consistent. If you are using fabric paint, fix (set) it with a hot iron, following the manufacturer's instructions.

OPPOSITE: Printing motifs on the blind and accessories as well as the walls creates a completely unified decorative scheme. If you prefer a more nature-inspired effect, print the leaves on the blind in green ink.

STARS AND STRIPES

All too often, creative decorating is restricted to the larger rooms of a house, but the hall is the first thing everybody sees when they come through the front door. Why not use stamping to make a stunning first impression on your visitors? This colour scheme combines two earth colours with bright silver stars to give a slightly Moroccan feel. If you have an immovable carpet or tiles that don't suit these shades, then choose a colour from your existing floor covering to highlight the walls. Hallways seldom have windows to give natural light and the inclination is to use light, bright colours to prevent them from looking gloomy. A better idea is to go for intense, dramatic colours with good electric lighting – they will turn a corridor into a welcoming hallway.

You will need

- household sponge
- emulsion (latex) paint in light coffee and spicy brown
- plumbline
- reusable adhesive
- straight-edged card (stock), the width required for the stamps
- pencil
- paintbrush
- scissors
- silver acrylic paint
- plate
- foam roller
- starburst stamp

1 Use a household sponge to apply irregular patches of light coffee emulsion (latex) paint to the wall. Aim for a mottled effect. Leave to dry.

2 Attach a plumbline at ceiling height with reusable adhesive so that it hangs just away from the wall. Line up one straight edge of the card (stock) and use it as a guide to draw a straight line in pencil down the wall.

3 Move the card marker one width space along the wall, and continue to mark evenly spaced lines. This will create the striped pattern.

4 Paint the first stripe spicy brown. Try to keep within the pencil lines, but don't worry too much about slight mistakes as the wall should look hand-painted and not have the total regularity of machine-printed wallpaper.

5 Continue painting each alternate stripe, keeping within the pencil lines, but attempting to create a slightly irregular finish.

6 Cut the card spacer to the length required to use as a positional guide for the stars. Spread some silver paint on to the plate and run the roller through it until it is evenly coated. Ink the stamp and print a star in each of the spicy brown stripes along the wall, above and below the card spacer. Continue printing across the wall, then return to the first stripe and start printing again, one space below the lowest star.

7 Using the card spacer as before, print the first two rows of stars in the coffee-coloured stripes. Position these stars so they fall midway between the stars in the spicy brown stripe.

8 Continue this process to fill in the remaining silver stars all down the coffee-coloured stripes.

RIGHT: Painting stripes on the wall gives a bold background for the silver stamped stars. You could try this technique with other motifs, for example diamonds. The stripes do not need to be perfectly accurate as the whole effect of the wall is intended to look hand-done rather than like mass-produced wallpaper.

HEAVENLY CHERUBS

The cherubs are stamped in silhouette on this wall, framed in medallions of pale yellow on a dove-grey background. The yellow medallions are stencilled on to the grey background and the combination of colours softens the potentially hard-edged dark silhouettes. The stencil can be cut from card (stock) or transparent mylar and the paint is applied with the same roller that is used for inking the stamps. The theme is extended to the painted wooden key box and the lampshade.

You will need

- emulsion (latex) paint in dove-grey, pale yellow and charcoal-grey
- household paintbrushes
- plumbline
- card (stock), 25 x 25cm/10 x 10in
- pencil
- ruler
- stencil card
- craft knife
- self-healing cutting mat
- plates
- foam rollers
- 2 cherub stamps and 1 swag stamp
- lidded wooden box
- fine-grade abrasive paper (sandpaper)
- cloth
- burnt-umber artist's oil colour
- cream fabric lampshade and ceramic lamp base
- black stamp pad
- scrap paper
- scissors
- masking tape

1 Paint the wall with dove-grey paint and leave to dry. Attach a plumbline at ceiling height, just in from one corner. Hold the card (stock) square against the wall so that the string cuts through the top and bottom corners. Mark all the corner points in pencil. Move the card and continue marking the wall to make a grid for the stamps.

2 Use a pencil and ruler to draw the medallion shape on a sheet of stencil card. Carefully cut out the stencil using a craft knife on a self-healing cutting mat. Spread pale yellow emulsion (latex) paint on to a plate and run the roller through it until it is evenly coated.

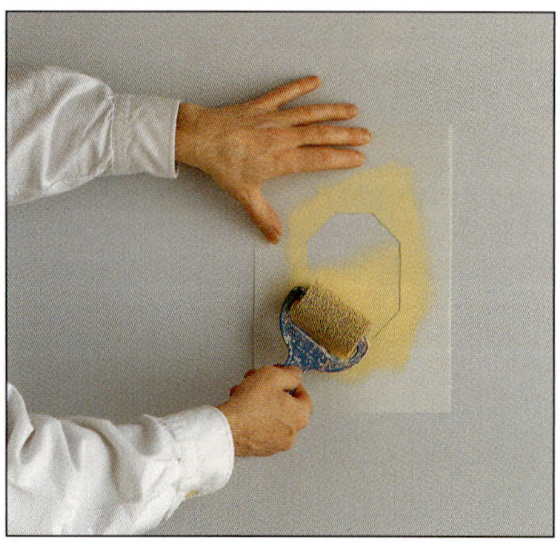

3 Position the stencil on one of the pencil marks and use the paint-covered roller to stencil the medallion shape. Paint all the medallions in this way, positioning the stencil in the same place on each pencil mark.

4 Ink one of the cherub stamps with charcoal-grey paint and make a print inside each medallion. Print the cherub in the centre.

5 Paint the wooden box with pale yellow emulsion (latex) paint, inside and out, and leave to dry.

6 Spread some charcoal-grey paint on to a plate and run a roller through it until it is evenly coated. Ink the second cherub stamp and make a print in the centre of the box lid. Print the swag stamp directly beneath the cherub.

7 Measure the sides of the box to determine the number of swag prints that will fit comfortably in a row. Mark the positions in pencil or judge by eye to add swags around the sides of the box. Leave to dry.

8 Rub the corners and edges of the box with fine-grade abrasive paper (sandpaper). Rub the prints in places to add a faded, aged look. Use a cloth to rub burnt-umber artist's oil colour on to the whole box, to give an antique appearance.

9 For the lampshade, stamp several swags on scrap paper and cut them out. Arrange the cut-outs on the lampshade to plan your design. Hold each piece in place with a small piece of masking tape.

10 Spread some dove-grey paint on to a plate and run a roller through it until it is evenly coated. Ink the swag stamp and print swags around the top of the lampshade, removing each paper motif in turn before you stamp in its place.

11 Continue stamping around the base of the shade in the same way, removing each paper motif in turn.

12 Stamp swags around the lamp base to complete the co-ordinated look. Judge the positioning by eye or use paper motifs as before.

RIGHT: Stencilled medallions give an extra dimension to the cherub wall design. The theme is continued with swags and cherubs on other items in the room.

MEDIEVAL DINING ROOM

Decorate your dining room using medieval patterns and colours that will make coming through the door a pleasure for you and your visitors. A dark colour above dado (chair) rail height creates the illusion of a lower ceiling, while a light colour below, combined with a light floor covering, seems to push the walls outwards to give the impression of width. The crown pattern is stamped in a diagonal grid, which is easy to draw using a plumbline and a square of card.

You will need

- pencil
- emulsion (latex) paint in dark blue-green, buttermilk yellow and light cream
- paintbrush
- fine-grade abrasive paper (sandpaper)
- masking tape
- ruler
- paint roller
- wallpaper paste (mixed following the manufacturer's instructions)
- plate
- diamond and crown stamps
- foam roller
- plumbline
- card (stock), 15 x 15cm/6 x 6in

1 Draw a horizontal pencil line on the wall, at dado (chair) rail height. Paint the top half of the wall in dark blue-green and the bottom in buttermilk yellow. When dry, lightly sand the blue-green paint. Stick a strip of masking tape along the lower edge of the blue-green, and another 10cm/4in below. Apply light cream paint with a dry roller over the buttermilk yellow.

2 Stick another length of masking tape 2cm/5in below the one marking the edge of the blue-green section. Using a paintbrush and blue-green paint, fill in the stripe between the two lower strips of tape. Leave to dry and peel off the tape. Lightly sand the blue-green stripe to give it the appearance of the upper section of wall.

3 On a plate, mix one part blue-green emulsion (latex) paint with two parts pre-mixed wallpaper paste and stir well. Ink the diamond stamp with the foam roller and stamp a row of diamonds on the narrow cream stripe.

4 Use the plumbline and card (stock) square to mark an all-over grid on the cream half of the wall. This will be used as a guide for the crown stamps.

ABOVE: A simple crown stamp is used here to dramatic effect. You could extend the medieval theme to furniture in the room, for example a wooden box or cabinet.

5 Ink the crown stamp with the blue-green emulsion and wallpaper paste mixture and stamp a motif on each pencil mark. Make several prints before re-inking to create variation in the density of the prints.

CHECKS AND CHERRIES WINDOW

Bring the flavour of the French countryside into your home with checks and cherries. These popular designs are found adorning all kinds of crockery, enamelware, fabrics, pelmets and furniture in rural France. The checked border is applied with an ingenious self-inking rubber roller stamp, which is so easy to use you could get carried away. Be careful, though, because too many checks could become overpowering. Stamp the cherries randomly to make an all-over pattern, leaving plenty of space between the prints in order to prevent the pattern from looking too busy. Keep the whole effect light and airy.

You will need

- masking tape or pencil and ruler
- square-tipped 2.5cm/1in paintbrush
- emulsion (latex) paint in corn-yellow
- scrap paper
- check-pattern self-inking blue rubber roller stamp
- red stamp pad
- cherry motif rubber stamp

1 Mark the border around the window frame, either applying masking tape along the outer edge or marking it with light pencil guidelines. Paint the border corn-yellow.

2 Mitre the corners for the roller stamp by positioning a sheet of scrap paper at a 45-degree angle, continuing the line of the mitred window frame. Hold the paper in place with tape.

3 Run the blue check-pattern roller stamp down, following the edge of the yellow border and overprinting the mitring paper. Do this in one smooth movement.

4 Flip the paper over, keeping the same angle, and run the roller stamp across the bottom of the border. Overprint the paper then remove it.

5 Use the red stamp pad and the cherry motif rubber stamp to make a well-spaced pattern all over the surrounding wall.

ABOVE: Give your kitchen a face-lift with this cheerful, brightly coloured design scheme. Complement the look with blue-and-white checked dishtowels.

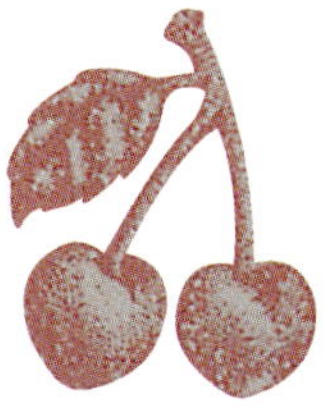

PROVENÇAL KITCHEN

This kitchen is a dazzling example of contrasting colours – the effect is almost electric. Colours opposite each other in the colour wheel give the most vibrant contrast and you could equally well experiment with a combination of blue and orange or red and green. If, however, these colours are just too vivid, then choose a gentler colour scheme with the same stamped pattern. The kitchen walls were colourwashed to give a mottled, patchy background. Put some wallpaper paste in the colourwash to make the job a lot easier – it also prevents too many streaks running down the walls. You can stamp your cabinets to co-ordinate with the walls.

You will need

- emulsion (latex) paint in deep purple and pale yellow
- wallpaper paste (made up according to the manufacturer's instructions)
- household paintbrush
- plumbline
- card (stock) approx. 30 x 30cm/12 x 12in
- pencil
- plates
- foam rollers
- rosebud and small rose stamps
- acrylic paint in red and green
- clear matt (flat) varnish and brush

1 To make the colourwash, mix one part deep purple emulsion (latex) with one part wallpaper paste and four parts water. Make it up in multiples of six. It is best to make more than you need. Colourwash the walls. If runs occur, pick them up with the brush and work them into the surrounding wall, aiming for a patchy, mottled effect.

2 Attach the plumbline at ceiling height, just in from the corner. Hold the card (stock) square against the wall so that the string cuts through the top and bottom corners. Mark all four points with a pencil. Continue moving the square and marking points to make a grid pattern.

3 Spread some deep purple paint on to a plate and run a roller through it until it is evenly coated. Ink the rosebud stamp and print a rosebud on each pencil mark until you have covered the entire wall.

4 If you wish to create a dropped-shadow effect, clean the stamp and spread some pale yellow paint on to a plate. Ink the stamp and overprint each rosebud, moving the stamp so that it is slightly off-register.

5 Continue overprinting the rosebud motifs, judging by eye the position of the pale yellow prints. This is known as a dropped-shadow effect.

6 For the cabinet doors, spread some green and red paint on to the plates and run the rollers through them until they are evenly coated. Ink the rose with red and the leaves with green. (If one colour mixes with the other, just wipe it off and re-ink.) Print a rose in the top left-hand corner.

RIGHT: The rosebud print is made to look more subtle by overprinting it in another colour slightly off-register.

7 Print the stamp horizontally and vertically to make a border along the edges of the door panel.

8 When you have printed round the whole border, leave the paint to dry. Apply a coat of clear matt (flat) varnish to protect the surface.

RIGHT: The traditional rosebud motif is given a new twist by printing it in unusual colours. Choose your own colour scheme to achieve the effect you want.

ROSE BREAKFAST ROOM

New homes are wonderfully fresh, but the perfectly even walls can look plain if you are used to details such as dado (chair) rails and deep skirting (base) boards. This project shows you how to retain the freshness of new pastel paintwork and add interest with a frieze at dado-rail height and a coat of colourwash below it. Don't worry about painting in a straight line for the frieze – just use two strips of low-tack masking tape and paint between them. You could even try doing it by hand, as it does add character to the decoration, even if you do wobble a bit! Wooden furniture is given a distressed paint finish in toning colours, and stamped with the rose designs to co-ordinate with the walls.

You will need

- abrasive paper (sandpaper)
- emulsion (latex) paint in cream, blue-green, dusky-blue and peach
- household paintbrushes
- cloth
- plates
- foam roller
- rosebud, small rose and large rose stamps
- scrap paper
- screwdriver (optional)
- wallpaper paste (made up according to the manufacturer's instructions)
- tape measure
- pencil
- masking tape
- spirit level
- straight-edged plank of wood
- square-tipped 2.5cm/1in artist's brush

1 To prepare the furniture, rub each piece down with abrasive paper (sandpaper) and apply a coat of cream paint. Make a blue-green glaze by diluting one part paint with three parts water, then brush it on following the direction of the grain. Before the paint has dried, use a cloth to wipe off some of the paint.

2 Spread the dusky-blue paint on to a plate and run the roller through it. Ink the rosebud stamp and print the design on to scrap paper.

3 Referring to the paper pattern, stamp the design in the centre of your chosen piece of furniture.

4 Stamp more rosebuds on either side of the central design. Work with the shape of the individual piece of furniture to decide upon the best position and the number of prints to use.

5 If you are decorating a desk or dresser, unscrew and remove any handles, then stamp the pattern on the drawer fronts. Screw them back after the paint has dried.

6 For a small piece of furniture like this chair, a simple design is best. Paint the chair with cream emulsion (latex) paint, then print a single small rose in peach.

7 To make the colourwash for the walls, mix one part peach emulsion (latex) paint with one part wallpaper paste and four parts water. Make it up in multiples of six. It is best to make more than you need, so that you can do the whole room from the same batch to ensure a colour match. Unless the room has been painted recently, apply a coat of cream emulsion to the walls.

8 Measure about 90cm/36in from the floor and make a pencil mark on the wall. Tape the spirit level to the plank and draw a straight line all round the room 90cm/36in above floor level. Draw another line 3cm/1¼in above it.

9 Apply the colourwash below the line using sweeping random brushstrokes. If runs occur, just pick them up with the brush and work them into the surrounding wall. Aim for a patchy, mottled effect.

10 If you have a steady hand, paint a dusky-blue stripe on the wall with the square-tipped brush, otherwise use masking tape to guide you and remove it when the paint is dry.

11 Spread the dusky-blue and peach paints on to the plates and use the foam roller or paintbrush to ink the large rose stamp, using the colours as shown. Print with the stamp base resting on the top of the dusky-blue stripe. Continue all round the room, re-inking the stamp each time for a regular print.

RIGHT: *Three rose stamps look very pretty used as a wall frieze and on matching painted furniture. This is an ideal way to decorate second-hand furniture.*

STARRY BEDROOM

At first glance, this bedroom looks wallpapered, but a closer examination reveals the hand-printed irregularity of the star stamps – some are almost solid colour while others look very faded. This effect is achieved by making several prints before re-inking the stamp. The idea is to get away from the monotony of machine-printed wallpaper, where one motif is the exact replica of the next, and create the effect of exclusive, hand-blocked wallpaper at a fraction of the price. The grid for the stars is marked using a plumbline and pencil. If you haven't got a plumbline, make your own by tying a key to a piece of string. You're bound to be delighted with the final result, and feel a great sense of achievement at having done it all yourself.

You will need

- sandy-yellow emulsion (latex) paint or distemper paint
- large paintbrush
- card (stock) 30 x 30cm/12 x 12in
- plumbline
- pencil
- brick-red emulsion paint
- plate
- foam roller
- folk-art star stamp

1 Paint the walls sandy yellow with emulsion (latex) paint or distemper paint. You may prefer a smooth, even finish or areas of patchy colour – each will create its own distinct look. Uneven colour will add to the effect of the uneven printing.

2 Hold the card (stock) square diagonally against the wall in the corner at ceiling height. Attach the plumbline at ceiling height so that the string cuts through the top and bottom corners of the square. Mark all four points with a pencil. Continue moving the square and marking points to form a grid all over the wall.

ABOVE: *Sunny colours give this bedroom a warm, welcoming feeling. The simple star design goes perfectly with traditional patchwork quilts and folk-art accessories. Country-style stamped furniture would also be at home in this room.*

3 Spread some brick-red paint on to the plate and run the roller through it until it is evenly coated. Ink the stamp and print a star on every pencil mark, or line the block up against each pencil mark to find your position, whichever you find easiest.

4 Experiment with the stamp and paint to see how many prints you can make before re-inking. Don't make the contrast between the pale and dark too obvious or the eye will always be drawn to these areas.

GRAPE BORDER BEDROOM

Who wouldn't want to sleep in this lovely lavender-grey and white bedroom? The choice of two cool colours has a very calming effect. The frieze is stamped in white at dado (chair) rail height around a lavender-grey wall. The simple reversal of the wall colours on the headboard provides both contrast and continuity. You can stamp on to an existing headboard or make one quite simply from a sheet of MDF (medium-density fiberboard) cut to the width of the bed. Use the stamps to make matching accessories in the same colours. For example, make the most of the stamps' versatility by using only the central part of the tendril stamp on the narrow border of a picture frame.

You will need

- drawing pin (thumbtack)
- string
- spirit level
- emulsion (latex) paint in white and lavender-grey
- plates
- foam rollers
- tendril, grape and leaf stamps
- headboard or sheet of MDF (medium-density fiberboard) painted white
- masking tape
- pencil
- ruler
- broad, square-tipped artist's paintbrush

1 Use a drawing pin (thumbtack) to attach one end of the string in a corner of the room at dado (chair) rail height. Run the string along the wall to the next corner and secure the end. Check the string with a spirit level and adjust if necessary.

2 Spread some white paint on to a plate and run a roller through it until it is evenly coated. Ink all three stamps and stamp a tendril, grape and leaf in sequence along the wall. Align the top edge of each stamp with the string and print below it.

3 When the first wall is complete, move the string to the next wall and continue all the way around the room. To decorate the headboard, stick masking tape around the top and side edges of the white board.

4 Spread some lavender-grey paint on to a plate and run a roller through it until it is evenly coated. Ink the leaf and tendril stamps. Align the stamp blocks with the masking tape and stamp alternate leaves and tendrils down both sides of the headboard.

5 Ink all three stamps and stamp a tendril, grape and leaf along the top edge of the headboard. Repeat the sequence to complete the row. Check the spacing before you stamp – wide spacing is better than the motifs appearing squashed together.

6 Measure a central panel on the headboard and lightly draw it in pencil. Stick strips of masking tape around the panel and the border. Mix some lavender-grey and white paint, then paint the border and the central panel in this pale grey colour.

RIGHT: Three stamps are used to create this beautiful border design. If you wish to decorate other pieces of bedroom furniture, you could use one or more of the stamps printed in groups or singly.

COUNTRY GRANDEUR BEDROOM

Redecorating a bedroom can be as refreshing as taking a holiday, and stamping is such fun that it won't seem like work at all. First sponge over a cream background with terracotta emulsion (latex) paint and add a final highlight of pink to create a warm, mottled colour. Any plain light-coloured wall can be covered in this way. The two stamps are then combined to make a border which co-ordinates with an all-over pattern on the wall and a bedside table. You can also decorate matching curtains and cushions, or stamp the border on sheets and pillowcases.

You will need

- emulsion (latex) paint in dark salmon-pink, off-white and dusky pink
- plates
- foam rollers
- fleur-de-lys and diamond stamps
- card (stock)
- plumbline
- pencil
- long ruler
- small table, painted off-white
- pair of compasses
- black stamp pad
- scrap paper
- scissors
- paintbrush
- clear matt (flat) varnish and brush

1 Spread some dark salmon-pink paint on to a plate and use a roller to ink the fleur-de-lys stamp. Stamp a row of fleurs-de-lys above the dado (chair) rail, using a piece of card (stock) 7.5cm/3in wide to space the motifs.

2 Ink the diamond stamp with the dark salmon-pink paint, and print diamonds between the fleur-de-lys motifs. Use a card spacing device if you are nervous about judging the positioning by eye.

3 Cut a card square about 25 x 25cm/10 x 10in. Attach a plumbline at ceiling height, just in from one corner so that the weighted end hangs down to the border. Use a pencil to mark a grid for the diamond stamps.

4 Ink the diamond stamp with the dark salmon-pink paint. Print a diamond on every pencil mark to make an all-over pattern.

5 Spread some off-white paint on to a plate and run a roller through it until it is evenly coated. Ink both stamps and overprint the border pattern. To create a dropped-shadow effect, stamp each print slightly below and to the left of the motif that has already been printed.

6 Overprint the diamond wall pattern in the same way.

7 Lay the ruler across the table top from corner to corner in both directions to find the central point. Mark the centre lightly in pencil.

8 Set the pair of compasses to a radius of 10cm/4in and lightly draw a circle in the centre of the table top.

9 Increase the radius to 12.5cm/5in. Position the point of the compasses on the edge of the circle, in line with the middle of the back edge of the table. Mark the point on the circle at the other end of the compasses, then move the point of the compasses to this mark. Continue around the circle to make five divisions. Connect the marks with light pencil lines to make a pentagonal shape.

10 Use the black stamp pad to print 15 diamonds on paper then cut them out. Arrange them around the pentagon, as shown. Use the compasses to mark the inner points of the five inward-pointing diamonds.

11 Spread some dusky pink paint on to a plate and run a roller through it until it is evenly coated. Ink the diamond stamp and print the five inward-pointing diamonds at the marked positions.

12 Re-ink the stamp as necessary and print the rest of the pattern. Print an arrangement of three diamonds in each corner of the table top. Paint any moulding and handles on the table in the same shade of pink. Seal the table with a coat of clear matt (flat) varnish.

RIGHT: Fleurs-de-lys and diamonds make an elegant combination. The circle of diamonds on the bedside table shows how a single simple motif can be positioned at different angles to create a complex design.

GREEK KEY BATHROOM

This bathroom looks far too elegant to have been decorated by an amateur. The border design is a classic Greek key interspaced with a bold square and cross. The black and gold look stunning on a pure white tiled wall. Every bathroom has different features, so use the border to make the most of the best ones, while drawing attention away from the duller areas. If you like a co-ordinated scheme, you could print the same border on a set of towels, using fabric inks.

You will need

- tracing paper
- pencil
- scissors
- spray adhesive
- high-density foam rubber, such as upholstery foam
- craft knife
- acrylic enamel paint in black and gold
- plates
- wooden batten (furring strip) 2–3cm/ $\frac{3}{4}$–$1\frac{1}{4}$in wide, depending on the bathroom
- scrap paper
- masking tape

1 Trace, transfer and cut out the pattern shapes from the template section. Lightly spray the shapes with adhesive and place them on the foam rubber. To cut out the shapes, cut the outline first, then undercut and remove any excess, leaving the pattern shape standing free of the foam rubber.

2 Spread an even coating of black paint on to a plate. Place the batten (furring strip) up next to the door frame to keep the border an even distance from it. Make a test print on scrap paper then begin by stamping one black outline square in the bottom corner, at dado (chair) rail height. Print a key shape above it, being careful not to smudge the adjoining edge of the previous print.

3 Continue alternating the stamps around the door frame.

4 Mark the baseline of the design area with masking tape and alternate the motifs along this line.

5 Spread a coating of gold paint on to a plate and dip the cross shape into it. Make a test print on scrap paper, then print the shape in the centre of square frames.

RIGHT: This design would look very dramatic stamped in plain black in a kitchen or bathroom.

SEASCAPE BATHROOM FRIEZE

This really is instant decorating. The sponge shapes come from a child's sea-life painting set. Other themed sets available include jungle, dinosaur, transport and farm animals. Although these are children's sponges, the project is not intended for an exclusively child-oriented bathroom scheme. The shapes are appropriate for grown-ups, too, and they can also be used to decorate other rooms in the home.

You will need

- ruler
- pencil
- spirit level
- emulsion (latex) paint in cream, brick-red and blue
- plates
- seashore-themed children's painting sponges
- scrap paper

1 Draw a line for the base of your frieze, using a ruler, pencil and spirit level. Spread the paints on to separate plates and press the sponge shapes into the paint following a sequence of cream, brick-red and blue. Make test prints on scrap paper to make sure that the sponges are not overloaded. Print all the sponge shapes across the baseline, then repeat the sequence to make another row.

2 Partially overprint each shape by dipping each sponge into a different colour from the one first used.

3 Continue overprinting the shapes. The second colour adds a shadow effect, giving the shapes a more three-dimensional appearance.

FURNITURE AND FURNISHINGS

Make it a rule never to pass by a second-hand furniture shop without glancing in. It's not that stamping is unsuitable for new furniture, just that doing up old junk is so rewarding. You are far less likely to experiment with a new chair than with one that actually needs some life breathing into it! Of course, there are always exceptions. White kitchen units, for example, can be given a new identity with matt (flat) oil-based paint. You can use emulsion (latex) paint on bare wood, and the designs can be protected with varnish. If the wood has previously been painted, use abrasive paper (sandpaper) to give the paint a matt texture to key into.

ABOVE: Stamping will transform a plain wooden or painted piece of second-hand furniture such as this kitchen chair.

LEFT: Choose from the many different ready-made stamps or make your own. Always use a separate brush for varnish.

EGYPTIAN TABLE TOP

The beauty of this table top design lies in its simplicity. Just one colour was used on a bold background, with three similar images stamped in regimented rows. The table used here has a lower shelf, but the design would work equally well on any occasional table. The salmon-pink prints show up well on the rich background, making it look even bluer. The stamps are pre-cut and are taken from Ancient Egyptian hieroglyphs. The finished table could be one element of a themed room, or the surprising and eye-catching centrepiece of a room decorated in subdued colours.

You will need

- 3 hieroglyphic rubber stamps
- ruler
- 2 card (stock) strips, for measuring stamp positions
- felt-tipped pen
- set square (triangle)
- emulsion (latex) or acrylic paint in salmon-pink
- small paint roller
- piece of card or plastic

1 Use the stamp blocks and a ruler to measure out the stamp positions. Place a card (stock) strip along the vertical edge of the table. Mark as many stamp lengths as will fit along it, leaving equal spaces between them. Work out the positioning carefully so that the rows of prints will fit comfortably. Use the second card strip to mark the widths of the stamps.

2 Place the horizontal measure across the table so that it marks the position of the first row. The top of the stamp will touch the measuring strip. Use a set square (triangle) to position the vertical strip at a 90-degree angle to the first row. Move the vertical strip along as you stamp. Coat the roller with paint by running it through a blob of paint on a spare piece of card or plastic.

3 Use the roller to coat the stamps, then print them in sequence all along the first row. Position the stamps following the marks you have made on the card strips.

4 Move the horizontal measure up one stamp space on the vertical measure and stamp a second row of figures. Once again, the tops of the stamps will touch the bottom of the horizontal strip. Check that the card measures remain at a 90-degree angle. Continue until the pattern covers the whole table top.

BELOW: Vibrant colours turn an ordinary table into a main feature. You could also use subtle colours such as beige and brown.

STARFISH BATHROOM CHAIR

Old wooden chairs are not expensive and, with a bit of careful hunting round second-hand shops, you should be able to find yourself a real bargain. Take the time to strip the old layers of paint – it might take some time, but it gives you a much better base to work on. This chair was given an undercoat of white emulsion (latex) paint, then it was dragged with yellow-ochre in the direction of the grain before being stamped with starfish motifs in light grey. Choose colours that complement your bathroom scheme so that your Starfish Bathroom Chair will blend in with the existing fittings.

You will need

- medium-grade abrasive paper (sandpaper)
- wooden chair
- emulsion (latex) paint in white, yellow-ochre and light grey
- household paintbrush
- plate
- foam roller
- starfish stamp
- clear matt (flat) varnish and brush

1 Sand or strip the chair, then apply a coat of white emulsion (latex) paint. Mix a thin wash of about five parts water to one part yellow-ochre emulsion. Use a dry brush to drag a little glaze at a time in the direction of the grain. Keep drying the brush as you work, to ensure you do not apply too much glaze.

2 Spread some light grey paint on to the plate and run the roller through it until it is evenly coated. Ink the starfish stamp and print around the edge of the chair seat so that the design overlaps on to the sides.

3 Fill in the seat area with starfish stamps, rotating the stamp to a different angle after each print. Space the stamps quite close together to make a dense pattern. Leave to dry thoroughly before applying a coat of varnish to protect the surface.

OPPOSITE: You can continue the starfish theme with a frieze on the wall.

BEACHCOMBER'S STOOL

If you stumble across a small milking stool like this one, don't hesitate, just buy it! These sorts of stools were, and still are, used in kitchens, gardens and worksheds for a whole range of tasks. Small children love to sit on them and adults find them invaluable when shelves are just out of reach. They can be used for weeding, sketching, fishing or any activity that requires being close to the ground but not actually on it. This second-hand shop find was painted orange before being stamped with the seashore pattern. It's just the thing to sit on while peeling prawns or cleaning mussels.

You will need

- small wooden stool
- emulsion (latex) paint in orange
- household paintbrush
- emulsion, acrylic or poster paint in deep red, purple and pale peach
- plates
- foam rollers
- shell, seahorse and starfish stamps
- water-based matt (flat) varnish and brush

1 Paint the stool orange and leave to dry. Spread some deep red paint on to a plate and run the roller through it until it is evenly coated. Ink the shell stamp and make a print in the centre of the stool.

2 Ink the seahorse stamp with purple paint and make a print either side of the shell print. The seahorses face the same direction.

3 Ink the starfish stamp with pale peach paint. Print a starfish border, overlapping the edge so that the design goes down the sides of the stool.

4 When the paint has dried, apply a coat of varnish to the stool. The varnish will dry to a matt (flat) sheen.

BELOW: For a more traditional nautical look, use shades of blue and turquoise.

FISH FOOTSTOOL

This low stool decorated with a leaping fish motif would look good in the bathroom or on the patio for drinks, or it could be used simply for putting your feet on. Any small and useful stool that looks handmade would be a suitable candidate for a make-over. The fish and border blocks are cut from high-density foam and the light and dark blue colour scheme is reminiscent of Balinese batik prints.

You will need

- small stool
- emulsion (latex) paint in dark blue, light blue and off-white
- household paintbrushes
- tracing paper
- pencil
- scissors
- spray adhesive
- high-density foam, such as upholstery foam
- craft knife
- scrap paper
- plate

1 Give the stool two coats of dark blue paint and leave to dry. Trace, transfer and cut out the two pattern shapes from the template section. Lightly spray the shapes with adhesive and place them on the foam. Cut around the outlines with a craft knife, then scoop out the pattern details.

2 Print five fish shapes on to scrap paper and cut them out. Use these to plan the position of the fish design on the stool. The fish should look as if they are swimming at different angles.

3 Spread some light blue and off-white paint on to a plate. Using a paintbrush, apply off-white paint to the top of the fish and light blue to the bottom. Make a test print on scrap paper to make sure the stamp is not overloaded.

4 Using the paper shapes as a guide, stamp the fish lightly on the surface of the stool, printing both colours at the same time.

BELOW: Stamping the fish at different angles gives a lovely illusion of life and movement – they seem to be swimming through deep blue water.

5 Paint the border stamp using the off-white paint. The border is intentionally ragged, so don't go for strict straight edges, but stamp the design in a slightly haphazard fashion.

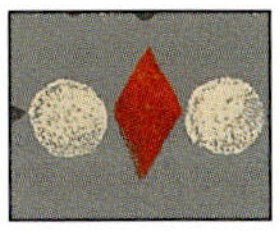

FOLK MOTIF CHAIR

Old kitchen chairs are functional and comfortable but often very plain. This modular style of decoration allows you to unite a non-matching set of chairs by stamping them with similar designs in the same colours. They will look much more interesting than a new set, and will have cost a fraction of the price.

You will need

- wooden kitchen chair
- emulsion (latex) paint in light blue-grey
- small household paintbrush
- abrasive paper (sandpaper) (optional)
- ruler
- pencil
- tracing paper
- scissors
- spray adhesive
- medium-density sponge
- craft knife
- plate
- acrylic or emulsion paint in red, white and dark blue-grey
- scrap paper
- clear matt (flat) varnish and brush

1 Give the chair at least two coats of light blue-grey paint and leave to dry. To achieve a "weathered" look, you could rub down the paint between coats, to let some of the grain show through. Use a ruler to find the centre of the back rest and make a small pencil mark. Trace, transfer and cut out the pattern shapes from the template section. Lightly spray the shapes with adhesive and place them on the sponge. Cut around the outlines with a craft knife.

2 Use a plate as your palette. Spread out an even coating of red, white and dark blue-grey acrylic or emulsion (latex) paint. Press the diamond shape into the red paint and make a test print on scrap paper. Stamp the diamond shape on the marked centre point of the back rest.

3 Stamp a white circle on either side of the diamond.

4 Stamp a dark blue-grey triangle and finally a red half-moon shape on either side of the stamped motifs, to form a symmetrical pattern.

5 Using the small square shape, stamp dark blue-grey diamonds around the edge of the back rest with equally sized gaps in between.

6 Stamp dark blue-grey squares on the back crossbar, as shown. Then fill in the gaps on the back rest with white diamonds and the gaps on the back crossbar with white squares.

7 Stamp dark blue-grey triangles, pointing outwards, to form a "sawtooth" border down both sides of the chair back.

8 Stamp red circles on the front legs where the lower crossbars meet them. Stamp dark blue-grey triangles above and below the circles, pointing outwards. Add some dark blue-grey and white diamonds to the centres of the lower crossbars. Finally, when all the paint is dry, give the whole chair a coat of clear matt (flat) varnish to protect the design.

GOTHIC CABINET

Visit second-hand shops to find old pieces of furniture with some interesting detailing and panels that would take a stamped heraldic design. This small bedside cabinet looked very gloomy with its original dark woodstain, but has shed its old image and become a complete extrovert as the centrepiece of a medieval entrance hall.

You will need

- small wooden cabinet
- fine-grade abrasive paper (sandpaper)
- emulsion (latex) paint in rust-brown, dark blue-green, lilac and yellow-ochre
- household paintbrush
- medium-sized artist's paintbrush
- black stamp pad
- diamond and fleur-de-lys stamps
- scrap paper
- scissors
- pencil
- ruler (optional)
- plates
- foam rollers
- red-orange smooth-flowing water-based paint (thinned emulsion, poster paint or ready-mixed watercolour)
- lining brush
- shellac and brush
- water-based tinted varnish
- fine wire (steel) wool

1 Sand away the existing varnish or paint. Paint the cabinet in rust-brown on the main body and dark blue-green on any carved details and on the panels. Use the artist's paintbrush to paint the blue-green right into the panel edges, to ensure even coverage.

2 Use the stamp pad to print the diamond and fleur-de-lys motifs on paper and cut them out. Lay them on the panels to plan your pattern. Make a small pencil mark on the panel at the base point of each motif as a guide for stamping. Use a ruler if necessary to make sure the design is symmetrical. Mark the base point of the motif on the back of each stamp block so that you can line up the marks when you print.

3 Spread some lilac paint on to a plate and run a roller through it until it is evenly coated. Ink the diamond stamp and print diamonds using the pencil marks as a guide.

4 Spread some yellow-ochre paint on to a plate and ink the fleur-de-lys stamp. Print the fleur-de-lys motifs, using the pencil marks as a guide.

5 Using red-orange paint and the lining brush, add hand-painted details to the motifs. Support your painting hand with your spare hand resting on the surface of the cabinet and aim to get a smooth, flowing line.

6 Apply a coat of shellac to seal the surface for varnishing and leave to dry. Apply a fairly thick coat of tinted varnish and leave to dry. Rub the raised areas and edges of the cabinet with fine wire (steel) wool to simulate natural wear and tear.

RIGHT: Hand-painted details in red-orange make these heraldic motifs look even more sumptuous. The rich colours are typical of the Gothic Revival furniture made popular by William Morris and the Arts and Crafts Movement in the 19th century.

STAR CABINET

This attractive little cabinet seems to fit in the moment you have finished it. While its style is individual, it does not scream out for attention, and it has that comfortable, lived-in look. The cabinet was painted, stamped, then painted again. Finally, it was given a coat of antiquing varnish and rubbed back with a cloth in places. It glows from all the attention and took just one afternoon to make. This style of decoration is so simple that you might consider transforming other items of furniture in the same way.

You will need

- wooden wall cabinet
- emulsion (latex) paint in olive-green, off-white and vermilion
- household paintbrushes
- plates
- tracing paper
- pencil
- scissors
- spray adhesive
- medium-density sponge, such as a kitchen sponge
- craft knife
- PVA (white) glue
- matt (flat) varnish in antique pine and brush
- kitchen cloth

1 Paint the cabinet with a coat of olive-green emulsion (latex) paint, applying a second coat if necessary.

2 Trace, transfer and cut out the star shape from the template section. Lightly spray with adhesive and place on the sponge. Cut out with a craft knife. Spread some off-white paint on to a plate. Dip the sponge star shape into the paint and print stars all over the cabinet, quite close together.

3 Make a mixture of two-thirds vermilion paint and one-third PVA (white) glue. When the stars have dried, coat the cabinet with a liberal amount of this colour, daubed on with a brush.

ABOVE: A simple design is made special by coating it with diluted paint and tinted varnish.

4 Finish the cabinet with a coat of tinted varnish, then use a cloth to rub some of it off each of the stars. This layering of colour gives the surface its attractive rich patina.

NONSENSE KEY CABINET

If you have a well-developed sense of the ridiculous, then this project will appeal to you. The idea is to use three totally unconnected images of varying scales to form a nonsense design. Our choice was three morris dancers below a large old-fashioned tap, surrounded by stars, but you can choose anything you like. The wooden cabinet was painted with white primer before the stamps were added in dark blue ink. The colour was applied with a fine artist's paintbrush using bright watercolour paint. The streaky paint finish was achieved with yellow watercolour wiped on with a small piece of sponge.

You will need

- small key cabinet
- white primer
- small household paintbrush
- selection of stamps
- permanent ink stamp pad in navy-blue
- scrap paper
- craft knife
- watercolour paints
- fine artist's paintbrush
- small piece of sponge
- medium-grade abrasive paper (sandpaper)
- clear matt varnish and brush (optional)

1 Apply two coats of white primer to the bare wood of the key cabinet, allowing the primer to dry thoroughly between coats.

2 Stamp a selection of motifs on to scrap paper and cut them out. Use them to plan your design by positioning the paper pieces on the central panel of the cabinet door.

3 When you are happy with your layout, stamp the designs directly on to the cabinet. Use the paper pieces as a guide by moving them out of the way at the last moment.

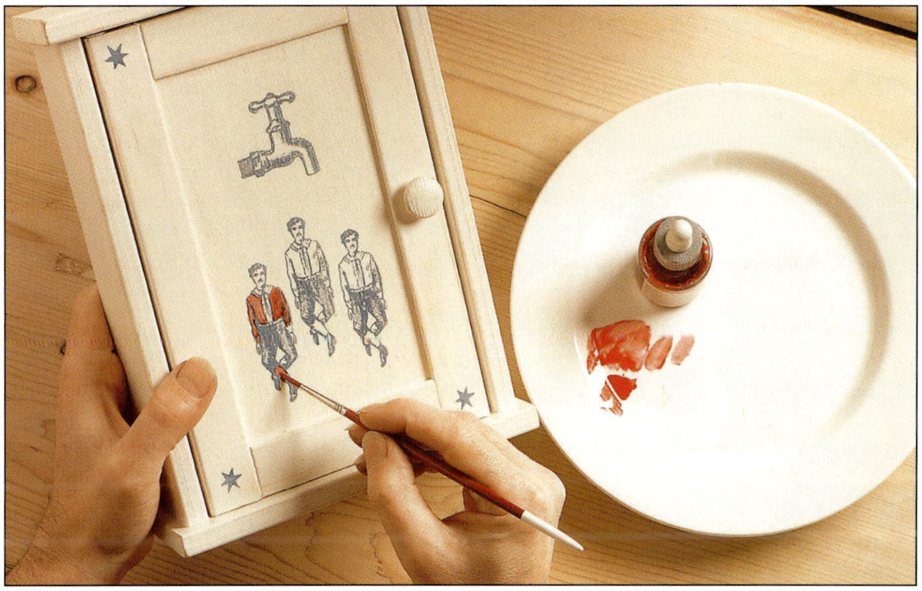

4 Stamp a small star in each corner of the cabinet door.

5 Begin to paint the details of the illustrated panel using watercolour paints and a fine artist's paintbrush. Fill in the first colour.

6 Continue filling in the details of the prints, adding more colour.

7 Complete the details and leave to dry. When the paint has dried, use a small piece of sponge to wipe yellow watercolour paint over the cabinet avoiding the central, nonsense-illustrated panel.

8 When the paint has dried, lightly rub down the yellow paint with abrasive paper (sandpaper). If desired, seal the surface with a coat of clear varnish.

RIGHT: For a quicker finish, leave the details and background unpainted. The combination of blue and white creates a more cooling effect than vibrant primaries.

COUNTRY CABINET

A popular designer's trick is to paint a piece of furniture in the same colours as the background of the room, but in reverse. This co-ordinates the room without being overpoweringly repetitive. A small cabinet like the one in this project is perfect for such a treatment. Don't be too precise in your stamping – a fairly rough-and-ready technique gives the most pleasing results.

You will need

- wooden cabinet
- emulsion (latex) paint in brick-red and yellow
- small household paintbrush
- plate
- foam roller
- small star stamp
- fine wire (steel) wool or abrasive paper (sandpaper)
- water-based matt (flat) varnish and brush

1 Paint the cabinet with a base coat of brick-red emulsion (latex) paint. Leave to dry.

2 Spread some yellow paint on to the plate and run the roller through it until it is evenly coated. Ink the stamp and print on to the cabinet.

3 Rub around the edges with wire (steel) wool or abrasive paper (sandpaper) to simulate natural wear and tear. This will give an aged appearance.

ABOVE: Rustic-coloured paints, a "distressed" finish and random stamping make this kind of furniture ideal for a country-style interior.

4 Apply a coat of varnish tinted with the brick-red paint (one part paint to five parts varnish) to tone down the contrast between the prints and the background paint.

FABRICS

Making patterns on fabric with rubber or foam stamps is not a new idea and many textiles from small rural communities are still handblocked today. At the other end of the market, very expensive, limited editions of "designer" textiles gain their value because of their labour-intensive style of production. There are a few important rules to obey with fabric: always wash it first; always use permanent inks (some need heat-sealing); and always work with a protective backing sheet under the fabric. Avoid fabrics which have special surfaces that will not absorb the ink and those with very loose weaves and furry materials. You should also avoid using fabric conditioner and starch.

ABOVE: Stamp simple motifs on ready-made items such as these mix-and-match cushion covers – there is no need for sewing!

LEFT: Special fabric paints are now available in a multitude of lovely colours. You will usually need an iron to fix (set) the paint.

FLEUR-DE-LYS CUSHIONS

A new set of cushions can instantly revive a tired decor or add a personal touch to a furnished apartment. If you are marking out your own territory, why not do it with vivacious colour contrasts for maximum impact? Choose hard-wearing medium-weight cotton cushion covers. Wash and iron the covers before decorating them and place a sheet of card (stock) inside each cover to protect the other side. The patterns used here are very much European in origin but the hemp fringing gives the cushions an unusual tropical flavour.

You will need

- fleur-de-lys, crown and diamond stamps
- black stamp pad
- scrap paper
- scissors
- 3 brightly coloured plain cotton cushion covers
- thin card (stock)
- pencil
- fabric paint in blue, orange and bright pink
- plates
- foam rollers
- long ruler
- iron
- hemp fringing, approximately 5.5m/6yd
- needle and thread or fabric glue

1 Print some fleurs-de-lys on paper and cut them out. Lay a cover on a work surface and arrange the motifs. Here, the bases of the motifs are 10cm/4in apart. Cut the card (stock) to the width of the space between the bases and about 7.5cm/3in high. Draw a line down the centre of the card.

2 Ink the stamp with the blue paint. Place the ruler across the fabric and rest the card on it. Print the first motif above the card. Move the card so that its top left-hand corner rests on the base of the first motif. Line up the centre of the stamp with the right-hand edge of the card to print the next.

3 Continue using the spacer card to print the first row of motifs. Move the ruler down for each new row, keeping it at a right angle to the edge of the cushion cover.

4 Print alternate rows so that the motifs fill the spaces left between the motifs in the row above. Print the other cushion covers using the same technique. Fix (set) the fabric paint with a hot iron, following the manufacturer's instructions. Attach hemp fringing around the covers.

ABOVE: For a more traditional look, use colours such as gold, maroon and cream.

AFRICAN-STYLE CUSHIONS

This glorious pile of cushions is a real stamper's fashion statement. The fabulous animal motifs create a distinctive African look. The stamps are perfect for making a themed set of cushions to display together. The covers are made from rough homespun fabric that has been vegetable-dyed in rich, spicy shades. The combination of the primitive stamped shapes and the textured fabric is very effective.

You will need

- fabric-stamping ink in black
- small rubber stamp for the borders
- 2 African-style rubber stamps
- sheet of thin card (stock)
- loose-weave cushion covers

1 Apply the fabric ink directly to the small border stamp and make a test print on a scrap of fabric to ensure that the stamp is not overloaded.

2 Place a sheet of card (stock) to fit inside the cushion cover. This will protect the other side from the black fabric ink.

3 Re-ink the stamp and print a row of small motifs round the edges of the cover to create a border.

4 Stamp a row of a larger motif at even intervals above the border. Use a combination of all three stamps in this way to complete the cushion design. Arrange the stamps in different ways on the other covers, either radiating out from the centre, or forming circles and squares.

BELOW: These unusual cushions show how you can build up quite different patterns using the same motifs. Experiment with other designs.

QUILTED CUSHIONS

A new pile of cushions can change the mood of a room in an instant – so why not update your living room or bedroom with these folk-inspired patterns? You can vary the star design on each cushion to make a co-ordinating mix-and-match set. Don't be daunted by the idea of quilting, as it really is very easy. Simply iron the backing, called quilter's wadding, on to the calico, then sew straight horizontal and vertical, or diagonal, lines through the centres of the stars. Alternatively, buy plain ready-made covers and stamp on the star patterns.

You will need

- 48 x 48cm/19 x 19in unbleached calico (washed and ironed)
- backing paper, such as thin card (stock) or newspaper
- fabric paint in brick-red and pear-green
- plates
- foam rollers
- folk-art star and small star stamps
- iron
- iron-on quilter's wadding
- needle and thread
- plain-coloured fabric, 48 x 48cm/19 x 19in, for the backing

1 Lay the calico on backing paper on a work surface. Spread some of the brick-red paint on to a plate and run the roller through it until it is evenly coated. Ink the folk-art star stamp.

2 Position the stamp in the corner of the calico and print. This square of calico will make the front of one cushion cover.

3 Continue stamping along the row, leaving a space the width of the stamp block between each print. Begin the next row with a blank space, and stamp the star so that it falls between the stars in the bottom row. Repeat these two rows of stars to cover the piece of calico.

4 Using the pear-green paint, ink the small star stamp and print between the red stars. Fix (set) the fabric paint with a hot iron, then iron on the wadding. Stitch horizontal and then vertical lines through the centres of the red stars. Place the calico and the backing fabric wrong sides together and machine stitch, leaving an opening.

ABOVE: These traditional folk-art designs would also look attractive stamped in shades of blue.

ROSE CUSHIONS

Don't get your needle and thread out for this project – just buy plain cushion covers and stamp them with contrasting colours. New cushions revitalize existing decor and they can change the mood of a room in an instant. They are also a clever way to distribute a themed pattern round a room as they subtly reinforce the rosy look. Natural fabrics like this thick cotton weave are perfect for stamping because they absorb the fabric paint easily to leave a good, sharp print. Fabric paints can be fixed (set) with a hot iron after applying to ensure a long-lasting and hard-wearing finish.

You will need

- sheet of thin card (stock)
- natural-fabric cushion covers in 2 different colours
- fabric paint in white and blue
- plates
- foam rollers
- rosebud, large rose and small rose stamps
- scrap paper
- scissors
- iron

1 Place the sheet of card (stock) inside the darker cushion cover. Spread some of the white fabric paint on to a plate and run the roller through it until it is evenly coated. Ink the rosebud stamp and make the first print in the bottom right-hand corner of the cover.

2 Continue stamping in rows, using the stamp block as a spacing guide – use the top edge as the position for the bottom edge of the next print. You should be able to judge by eye after a couple of prints. Fill the cover with a grid pattern of rosebuds.

3 For the second, paler-coloured cushion cover, ink all three stamps with the blue fabric paint. Stamp each one on to scrap paper and cut them out. Use the paper patterns to work out the position of the rows of motifs.

4 Re-ink the large rose stamp and make the first print in the top left-hand corner. Use the paper pattern to help with the spacing between the motifs. Complete the row.

5 Ink the small rose stamp and complete the next row, again using the paper pattern for spacing.

ABOVE: Fabrics with woven stripes make it very easy to position the rose prints, and add to the overall effect.

6 Stamp another row of large roses, then print the rosebud stamp in the same way to complete the pattern. Finally, fix (set) the fabric paints on both covers with a hot iron, following the manufacturer's instructions.

WHITE LACE PILLOWCASES

Attractive lace-edged pillowcases are now mass-produced and imported at very reasonable prices. You can buy many different designs ranging from hand-crocheted cotton to broderie-anglaise style cutwork. Choose a selection of different lace cushions, then stamp on top of them with delicate pink hearts to make a romantic display for the bedroom. Fabric paints work very well on cotton fabric, but it is advisable to wash and iron the pillowcases before you stamp them. This removes the glaze that might block the paint's absorption.

You will need

- lace-edged, white pillowcases
- iron
- ruler
- pencil
- sheet of thin card (stock)
- fabric paint in pale pink
- plate
- foam roller
- small heart stamp

1 Wash and iron the pillowcases to give a crisp, flat surface and remove any dressing in the fabric.

2 Using a ruler, measure between the corners to find the centre of the pillowcase. Make a small pencil mark at this point.

3 Place the sheet of card (stock) inside the pillowcase between the two layers so that the colour does not pass through to the other side.

4 Spread some pale pink fabric paint on to the plate and run the roller through it until it is evenly coated, then ink the small heart stamp. Print a group of four hearts so that the points meet at the central pencil mark.

5 Stamp another four hearts in line with the first, but with the points facing outwards. Leave to dry before fixing with a hot iron according to the manufacturer's instructions.

BELOW: *Experiment with other patterns using different heart stamps to make alternative versions of the lace pillowcase.*

TUMBLING ROSE CHAIR COVER

Ready-made slip covers for director's and wicker chairs provide an innovative way of restyling a room. It is rather like putting on a new jacket and changing your image. The design of the roses follows the curve of the chair and the direction of the seat. One of the advantages of these covers is that you can use them to disguise less than perfect chairs that are still structurally sound. Look out for old Lloyd loom chairs with sprung seats – their appearance may have been spoiled by coats of gloss paint over the years, but they're still ideal for a slip cover.

You will need

- fabric paint in green and red
- plate
- foam rollers
- large rose stamp
- ready-made calico slip cover
- sheet of thin card (stock)
- iron

1 Spread some green and red paint on to the plate and run the rollers through them until they are evenly coated. Ink the rose part of the stamp red and the stalk and leaves green.

2 Place the sheet of card (stock) behind the front panel of the slip cover and begin stamping the roses. Rotate the stamp in your hand after each print to get the tumbling rose effect.

3 Place the sheet of card behind the seat section and stamp the roses in the same way as the front.

4 Place the sheet of card inside the top section and stamp the top row, following the shape of the slip cover. Continue stamping to fill the cover, rotating the stamp as you did before. Fix (set) the fabric paint with a hot iron, following the manufacturer's instructions.

ABOVE: Tumbling roses would also look very pretty stamped on bedroom curtains or a large laundry bag.

COUNTRY-STYLE THROW

It's hard to imagine a home without a throw. Throws not only hide a multitude of sins like stains and worn patches, but they can instantly change the mood of a room with their colours and patterns. A casually draped throw gives off a wonderful sense of relaxation and comfort. The textured throw used in this project illustrates how well stamp prints can work on all sorts of surfaces, and most fabrics would be suitable. Fabric paints are easy to use, in fact most fabrics absorb the colour instantly, which means there is less chance of smudging than there would be on a smooth, non-porous surface such as wood or shiny paper. Always use a piece of backing paper when printing on fabric.

You will need

- plain-coloured throw, or suitable length of fabric with a hemmed edge
- iron
- backing paper, such as thin card (stock) or newspaper
- fabric paint in red, blue and purple
- plate
- paintbrush
- foam roller
- trellis heart stamp
- sheet of scrap paper

1 Press the throw or length of fabric with a hot iron so that it lies flat. Place it on some backing paper on a large work surface such as a wallpaper-pasting table.

2 Put the three fabric paints on to the plate and mix them together to create a violet-blue colour. Run the roller through the paint until it is evenly coated, then ink the stamp.

3 Starting in the top left-hand corner, about 4cm/1½in in from the edge, stamp a row of hearts. If you don't have a chequerboard pattern to follow, space them about 5cm/2in apart. Stamp the next row between the hearts in the first row. Overlap the rows by 2cm/¾in.

4 Take the design right up to the edge, printing part of the heart where it overlaps the edge. Have a sheet of scrap paper in place to take up the unwanted paint. Leave the design to dry before fixing (setting) it with a hot iron, following the manufacturer's instructions.

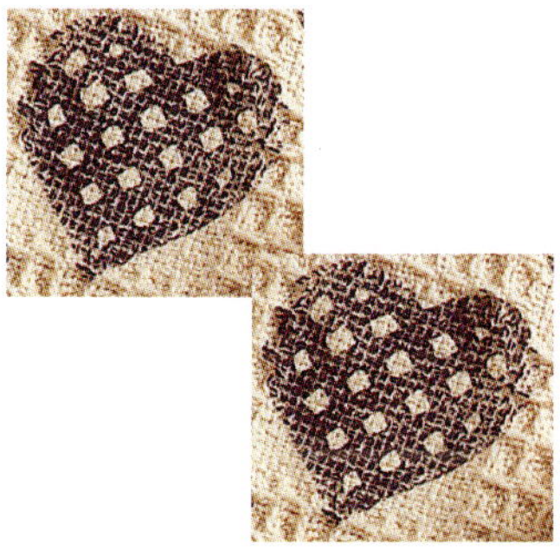

RIGHT: The textured fabric of this throw complements the pattern on the trellis hearts beautifully. It also helps you to position the stamp.

SEASHORE THROW

Throws are indispensable accessories in every home – while adding glorious swatches of colours to any room, they also cleverly disguise any worn or stained patches. Throws can be thick and wintry or light and airy like this one, which could also double up as a sarong for a quick wrap-around. Crêped cotton has a fine, crinkled texture, which adds volume to the fabric and makes it drape well. Cotton or other natural fibres are the best choice as they absorb the fabric paint easily. So, have a go at this throw and make a luxurious gold design for your home.

You will need

- backing paper, such as thin card (stock) or newspaper
- length of crêped cotton or a ready-made plain throw
- drawing pins (thumbtacks)
- fabric paint in gold
- plate
- foam roller
- seahorse and shell stamps
- iron

1 Protect your work surface with backing paper. Lay the crêped cotton fabric over this and pin down with drawing pins arond the edges.

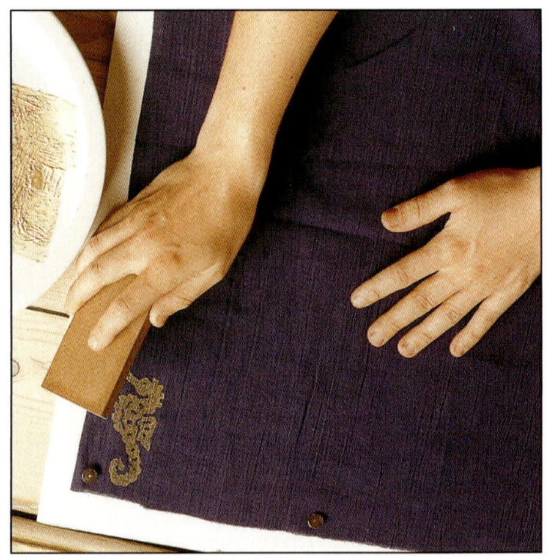

2 Spread some gold fabric paint on to the plate and run the roller through it until it is evenly coated. Ink the seahorse stamp and make the first print in one corner of the fabric.

3 Print a border along the top and bottom edges of the fabric, alternating the shells and seahorse stamps.

4 Stamp widely spaced rows of seahorses between the borders, turning the stamp 180 degrees each print. The prints in each row should fall between those of the previous row. Fix (set) the fabric paint with a hot iron, following the manufacturer's instructions. Press directly down on to the fabric, ensuring the crêped cotton retains its texture.

ABOVE: *Stamping is possible on many different fabrics, even the crinkled surface of crêped cotton.*

NO-SEW STAR CURTAIN

This is a quick and stylish solution to window dressing, especially if you don't like sewing. Light muslin (cheesecloth) drapes beautifully and its transparency allows the star pattern to show through the gathered layers. The motif is cut from medium-density sponge which is quite absorbent and makes several prints before you need to re-charge your stamp. You can use gold fabric paint but a more brilliant, glittering result is achieved by mixing bronze powder into a PVA (white) glue and water base.

You will need

- pencil
- tracing paper
- scissors
- spray adhesive
- medium-density sponge, such as a kitchen sponge
- felt-tipped pens
- craft knife
- bowl
- PVA (white) glue
- bronze powder
- paintbrush
- plate
- sheet of paper, the width of the muslin
- white butter muslin (cheesecloth)

1 Trace, transfer and cut out the pattern shape from the template section. Lightly spray the shape with adhesive and place it on the sponge. Draw around it in felt-tipped pen.

2 Cut out the star shape with a craft knife. First cut around the outline, then part the sponge and cut all the way through.

3 Mix up the gold colour in a bowl, using two spoonfuls of PVA (white) glue to one spoonful of water and half a spoonful of bronze powder. You can make a large or small amount of the mixture, just keep the proportions the same. Spread an even coating of the gold mixture on the plate.

OPPOSITE: This lovely airy window dressing could also be stamped with romantic cherubs.

4 Place the paper underneath the muslin (cheesecloth). Make a test print to ensure that the sponge is not overloaded, then print the first star just in from the corner. Measure the position of the next stamp with the width of three or four splayed fingers.

5 Measure upwards in the same way, and print the first star of the second row. This should be evenly spaced between the first two stars on the first row. Continue in this way, alternating the two rows, until you have covered the whole of the muslin fabric with evenly spaced stars.

SPRIGGED CALICO CURTAINS

Natural calico has a lovely creamy colour, especially when the sun shines through it. However, it is usually used as an upholsterer's lining fabric and this association can make calico curtains look unfinished. This stamped floral sprig lifts the humble calico into another dimension, giving it a sophisticated finish. Calico is prone to shrinkage, so wash the fabric before you stamp it and make up the curtains. Refer to the section at the beginning of the book for instructions for making the linocut stamp. You will find the sprig pattern in the template section.

You will need

- calico fabric
- backing paper, such as thin card (stock) or newspaper
- linocut stamp
- fabric stamping ink in green and dark blue
- scrap paper
- scissors
- ruler
- card (stock)
- pencil

1 Lay the fabric out on a flat surface, such as a wallpaper-pasting table, with the backing paper underneath. Make several prints of the linocut stamp on scrap paper, cut these out and use them to plan the position of the motifs on the fabric.

2 Decide on the distance between the sprigs and cut out a square of card (stock) with the same dimensions to act as a measuring guide. Use it diagonally, making a pencil mark at each corner all over the surface of the fabric.

3 Apply green ink directly to the edges of the linocut stamp.

4 Fill in the middle of the stamp with dark blue ink. Make an initial print on a scrap of fabric to determine the density of the stamped image.

5 Stamp the floral sprig on to the calico, using the pencil marks to position the base of the stamp. You need to apply gentle pressure to the back of the stamp and allow a couple of seconds for the ink to transfer. Don't rush; the result will be all the better for the extra time taken.

RIGHT: Calico tie-backs can be made to match the main fabric. You may find it easier to make the tie-backs before stamping, to determine the best position for the design.

STELLAR TABLECLOTH

These rubber stamps are the perfect way to add a heavenly aspect to your dining table, and it could not be easier to achieve. Fabric or paper napkins can be stamped to match the tablecloth. The tablecloth used here has a scalloped edge which makes for very easy spacing – simply count the scallops and then decide to stamp on, say, every third one. If you have a straight-edged cloth, measure the length and width of the cloth, and the length and width of the stamp to discover how many will fit comfortably along the edge. If the cloth isn't very big, find the centre by folding it in half and then in half again. Begin with a print at each corner, then one at the halfway mark, and space the other prints in between.

You will need

- tablecloth
- small and large star rubber stamps
- fabric-stamping ink in navy blue

1 Plan the position of your motifs, using one of the methods described above. Coat the smaller stamp with fabric ink and make a test print on to a scrap of fabric to ensure that the stamp is not overloaded.

2 Make the first print by positioning the small star rubber stamp in one corner of the tablecloth.

3 Stamp a large star on either side of the small star. Continue along the edges of the tablecloth, alternating the sizes of the stars.

4 Stamp one widely spaced square of small stars approximately 10cm/4in in from the first row (depending upon the size of your cloth) and then another square of large stars another 10cm/4in closer to the centre. It should look like an all-over pattern with a border.

ABOVE AND RIGHT: Scalloped edges and star motifs create a contemporary look for a dining room or occasional table.

STARFISH HAND TOWELS

These seashore-style hand towels are made from a cotton/linen mix, similar to the fabric used for glass cloths. Fabric paints are ideal for the job because the colour is permanent once fixed with an iron and you can use the towels again and again. The stamps have been given a three-dimensional look by stamping firstly in green and then overprinting some areas in white.

You will need

- pair of cotton/linen hand towels
- iron
- backing paper, such as thin card (stock) or newspaper
- fabric paint in green and white
- plate
- foam roller
- starfish and seahorse stamps

1 Wash the towels to remove any glaze from the fabric as this may block the absorption of the colour. Press each towel flat with an iron.

2 Place a towel on the backing paper. Spread some green paint on to the plate and run the roller through it until it is evenly coated. Ink the stamps and print a border, alternating starfish with seahorses.

3 Stamp two rows of green starfish down the length of the towel. Ink half the stamp edges with white paint. Overprint each stamped starfish and seahorse by lining up one point of the stamp with the green stamped image, then positioning the rest of the stamp.

LEFT: Making and decorating your own hand towels is surprisingly simple, and the towels will be very pleasant to use.

VINEYARD TABLE NAPKINS

These stamped table napkins look great with rush mats on a wooden table top. They bring together even the most casual collection of plates, glasses and cutlery to look like a deliberate choice. You can buy a set of plain table napkins or make your own by sewing straight seams along the edges of squares of cotton fabric. The fabric paints can be heat-treated with a hot iron to make the pattern permanent. Always follow the manufacturer's instructions, which may vary from brand to brand.

You will need

- terracotta-coloured table napkins
- iron
- newspaper
- cream-coloured fabric paint
- plate
- foam roller
- grape and tendril stamps

1 Wash and iron the napkins to remove any glaze which may block the paint's absorption. Lay the first napkin on top of several sheets of newspaper. Spread some cream fabric paint on to a plate and run the roller through it until it is evenly coated. Ink the grape stamp and print a bunch of grapes in each corner of the napkin.

2 Stamp a bunch of grapes halfway along each edge, then ink the tendril stamp and print tendrils between the grapes. Stamp all the napkins in this way and leave to dry. Seal the designs with an iron, following the paint manufacturer's instructions.

LEFT: You could stamp a tablecloth border to match the napkins.

STARRY FLOORCLOTH

A floorcloth is a sheet of canvas, painted and varnished and used in place of a rug. Canvas is hard-wearing, especially after a few coats of varnish, and it feels cool and smooth underfoot. Artist's canvas comes in all widths – just think of the paintings you've seen – and it is available through arts and crafts suppliers.

You will need

- plain cream artist's canvas
- pencil
- ruler
- scissors
- fabric glue and brush
- white acrylic primer
- household paintbrush
- emulsion (latex) paint in dark blue, lime-green and light blue
- plate
- foam roller
- starburst stamp
- matt (flat) varnish and brush

1 Draw a 4cm/1½in border around the edge of the canvas, then fold this back to make a seam. Mitre the corners by cutting across them at a 45-degree angle, then apply the glue and stick down the edges. Prepare the canvas by painting it with white acrylic primer.

2 Paint the primed floorcloth dark blue, applying two coats if necessary. Measure and draw a 10cm/4in border around the edge.

3 Paint the border lime-green, applying two coats to give a good coverage.

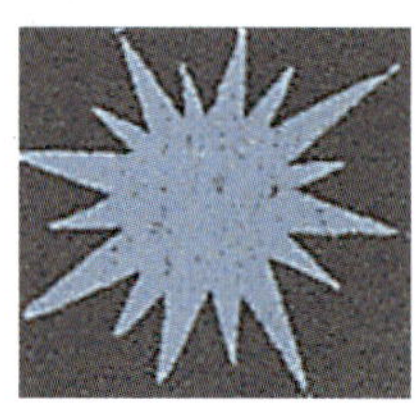

4 Spread some light blue paint on to the plate and run the roller through it until it is evenly coated. Ink the stamp and begin printing the stars in one corner. Judge the spacing visually, stamping a random arrangement of stars to cover the cloth.

5 Apply several coats of matt (flat) varnish, leaving each one to dry thoroughly before applying the next.

RIGHT: Create your own colour scheme to complement the furnishings in the rest of the room.

ROSE FLOORCLOTH

Here is an unusual alternative to buying an expensive runner-rug – simply make a floorcloth out of plain artist's canvas. Floorcloths were originally used by American settlers who found that sailcloth could be stretched over a bed of straw to cover their hard floors, and make an inexpensive and hard-wearing surface. They decorated them to imitate chequered marble floors and fine carpets, and found that the paint and varnish added to their durability. They were eventually replaced by the invention of linoleum, but have recently come back into fashion. Artist's canvas comes in many widths and is available through arts and crafts suppliers.

You will need

- plain cream artist's canvas (cut to the required size)
- pencil
- ruler
- scissors
- fabric glue and brush
- white acrylic primer
- paintbrush
- emulsion (latex) paint in black
- plate
- foam roller
- rosebud, small rose and large rose stamps
- large sheet of paper

1 Draw a 4cm/1½in border around the edge of the canvas, then fold this back to make a seam. Mitre the corners by cutting across them at a 45-degree angle, then apply the fabric glue and stick the seams down flat. Turn the canvas over and paint with one or two coats of white acrylic primer.

2 Spread some black paint on to the plate and run the roller through it until it is evenly coated. Ink all the stamps and print a circular repeat pattern on to the paper. You could use a plate to help draw an accurate circle.

3 Stamp six small roses along the bottom edge of the floorcloth, three in each corner. Place them at an angle, as shown.

4 Place the paper pattern over the floorcloth and lift it up as you stamp each element of the pattern on to the canvas. After you have printed the first rose circle pattern, you will get to know the order of the prints, and you may not need to refer to the paper pattern so often.

5 Leave the first completed circle to dry thoroughly before placing the paper pattern on to the next section and stamping the pattern as before. When you have repeated the pattern along the length, finish off the top edge of the floorcloth with the same six small roses that you started with.

RIGHT: A single circle of roses would look very attractive stamped in the centre of a tablecloth, using fabric paint.

CHERUB SHOPPING BAG

Large canvas shopping bags with shoulder straps are both fashionable and useful. They come in a range of plain colours that seem to cry out to be given an individual touch. Stamping works well on canvas and you can choose from fabric paint, acrylics or household emulsion (latex) paint. Bear in mind that you will not be able to wash the bag if you use emulsion or acrylic, while fabric paint can be fixed (set) with an iron to make it permanent and washable.

You will need

- blue canvas shopping bag
- backing card (stock)
- cherub and swag stamps
- black stamp pad
- scrap paper
- scissors
- emulsion (latex), acrylic or fabric paint in white and pale blue
- plate
- foam roller
- iron (optional)

1 Lay the bag on a flat surface and insert the backing card (stock) to prevent the paint from passing through to the other side.

2 Make several cherub and swag prints on scrap paper using the black stamp pad. Cut them out and arrange them on the bag to plan your design.

3 Spread some white paint on to the plate and run the roller through it until it is evenly coated. Ink the cherub and swag stamps and print the pattern, removing each paper motif and stamping in its place. Leave to dry, then ink the edges of the stamps with pale blue paint. Overprint the white design to create a shadow effect. If using fabric paint, follow the paint manufacturer's instructions to fix (set) the design with an iron.

TWO-TONE SCARF

Wrap yourself in garlands of roses by stamping a silk scarf with this red and green pattern. Scarves are wonderfully versatile and they really can make an everyday outfit look very special. When you're not wearing your scarf, drape it over a chair or hang it on a peg to add dashes of colour to a room. The scarf shown here was originally cream but it was then dipped in pink dye for an attractive two-tone effect – a light-coloured scarf would work just as well, though.

You will need

- fabric paint in red and green
- plates
- foam rollers
- small rose and rosebud stamps
- sheet of white paper
- silk scarf
- backing paper

1 Spread the red and green paint on to the plates and run the rollers through them until they are evenly coated. Ink the small rose red and its leaves and the rosebud stamp green. Stamp them on the corner and edges of the paper. Slip the paper pattern under the scarf on top of the backing paper.

2 Print alternating small roses and rosebuds around the border.

3 Fill in the middle of the scarf with two parallel rows of small roses.

TRAILBLAZER SCARF

Beginners are often nervous about printing on fabric for the first time. Here is a no-risk method of fabric printing which allows you to make all the design decisions and complete the stamping before you go near the fabric. The stamp is inked with fabric-transfer colour and the pattern laid out on paper first. The paper is then placed face-down on the fabric and a light pressure is applied to the back with a heated iron. When the paper is removed, the design will be transferred to the fabric in reverse. If you are still hesitant, rest assured that the printing must be done on synthetic fabric, so the project is relatively inexpensive.

You will need

- scarf in synthetic fabric
- thin white paper
- scissors
- 3 different rubber stamps
- transfer inkpads in red, blue and green
- iron

1 Measure the width of the scarf and cut paper strips of the same length. Make a border along each paper strip, using two alternating stamps and the red and blue inkpads. You will need four borders.

2 Cut a piece of paper to fit in the central area of the scarf. Stamp a widely spaced pattern using the third stamp and the green inkpad.

3 Place the scarf on a flat surface and turn the stamped paper patterns face-down in position along all four edges to make a border.

BELOW: Choose your own favourite motifs and colour scheme to make a scarf to match a particular outfit.

4 Apply light pressure with a dry iron, following the manufacturer's instructions on timing and temperature. Lift the iron between motifs – a sliding iron will blur your print.

5 Transfer the central pattern with the iron in the same way.

ANGEL T-SHIRTS

Fabric paints are very easy to use, come in a wide range of colours and can be fixed (set) with a hot iron to make them washable and permanent. The cherubs can be used in many ways, including the funky colour combinations chosen here. Strong contrasts, complementary shades or dayglo colours will all give the cherub motif a new image. By overprinting the cherubs slightly off-register in a second colour, you can add a three-dimensional look, too. Wash and iron the T-shirt before printing to remove any glazes that may block the absorption of the fabric paint.

You will need

- plain-coloured T-shirts
- backing card (stock)
- cherub and swag stamps
- black stamp pad
- scrap paper
- scissors
- fabric paint in various colours
- plate
- foam roller
- ruler (optional)
- iron

1 Lay a T-shirt on a flat surface and insert the backing card (stock) to prevent the paint from passing through to the other side.

2 Stamp several cherubs or cherubs and swags on scrap paper. Cut them out and arrange them on the T-shirt to plan your design.

3 Spread some fabric paint on to a plate and run the roller through it until it is evenly coated. Ink the cherub stamp and print the pattern, removing each paper motif and stamping a cherub in its place. Re-ink the stamp after each print and press down firmly with the stamp to allow the fabric paint to penetrate the fabric.

4 Use a ruler to help align the pattern if necessary. Stamp swag motifs around the neckline, if desired. Follow the paint manufacturer's instructions to fix (set) the design with an iron.

BELOW: *Experiment with other stamps and colours to create your own individual T-shirts for family and friends.*

CHINA AND GLASS

Stamping a motif gives the same print every time and this will enable you to make matching sets of crockery and glassware. Several brands of paint on the market are designed to be used on these surfaces at home. They don't need firing in kilns at high temperatures, but the paint can be made more resilient by baking in a domestic oven. The one drawback is that this paint is not recommended for food use, which means avoiding mouth contact, so don't paint around the lip of a glass or cup. Ceramic paints or acrylic enamels make crisp, opaque prints which are particularly effective on glass. Stamping is a perfect way to turn the jars from kitchen waste into kitchen accessories.

ABOVE: Humble utilitarian objects such as flowerpots will be transformed with colourful stamped borders and motifs.

LEFT: Acrylic enamel paint is used for stamping on both china and glass. Curved glass surfaces are best printed with foam stamps.

GOTHIC DISPLAY PLATE

Large china display plates look great mounted on the wall and they don't have to be confined to country kitchen-type interiors, as demonstrated by this bold pattern. The plate used here is a larger platter with a pale blue border outlined in navy blue, although the design can also be stamped on a plain plate. Use acrylic enamel paint to stamp on ceramics and glassware. It can be baked in a household oven according to the manufacturer's instructions. The resulting patterns are very hard-wearing and even seem to stand up to dishwashers and scouring pads, but the paints are recommended for display rather than for food use.

You will need

- black stamp pad
- diamond and crown stamps
- scrap paper
- scissors
- display plate
- acrylic enamel paint in navy blue and deep orange
- plates
- foam rollers
- ruler

1 Use the stamp pad to print eight diamond motifs and one crown on paper and cut them out. Arrange them on the plate to plan the design of the border pattern and central motif.

2 Spread some navy blue acrylic enamel paint on to a plate and run a roller through it until it is evenly coated. Ink the diamond stamp, then remove one of the paper shapes and stamp a diamond in its place.

OPPOSITE: Choose a display plate with a wide border and select a diamond stamp that will fit neatly inside it.

3 Place a ruler under the plate, so that it runs centrally from the printed motif to the one opposite. Line up the stamp with the edge of the ruler to print the second motif. Print diamond motifs on the other two sides of the plate in the same way, then fill in the diamonds in between, judging by eye.

4 Ink the crown stamp with deep orange paint and stamp a single crown in the centre of the plate. Bake the plate in the oven, following the paint manufacturer's instructions.

GRAPE JUG

A white ceramic jug (pitcher) like this one seems to be crying out for some stamped decoration, and the grape vine stamps do the trick in minutes. Choose a well-proportioned plain jug and transform it into something that is decorative as well as practical. Acrylic enamel paint is relatively new on the market and, although it resembles ordinary enamel, it is in fact water-based and does not require harmful solvents for cleaning brushes and stamps. Follow the manufacturer's instructions to "fire" the stamped jug in a domestic oven to add strength and permanence to the pattern. Without "firing", the paint will only stand up to non-abrasive cleaning.

You will need

- white ceramic jug (pitcher)
- detergent and clean cloth
- grape, tendril and leaf stamps
- black stamp pad
- scrap paper
- scissors
- acrylic enamel paint in black and ultramarine blue
- plate
- foam roller

1 Wash the jug (pitcher) in hot water and detergent, then wipe dry with a clean cloth to ensure that there is no grease on the surface.

2 Print a grape, a tendril and a leaf on to scrap paper and cut them out. Arrange them on the jug to plan the finished design.

3 Mix together the black and ultramarine blue acrylic enamel paint on a plate. Run the roller through the paint until it is evenly coated and ink the stamps. Stamp the motifs following your planned arrangement as a guide.

4 The leaf stamp may be used to fill any gaps, and the pattern may be repeated on the other side of the jug. Follow the manufacturer's instructions if you wish to make the design permanent by "firing" it in the oven.

RIGHT: For a more naturalistic effect, stamp the grapes in purple and the leaves and tendrils in green.

PERSONALIZED FLOWERPOTS

Commercially decorated flowerpots can be very expensive but you can customize ordinary clay pots very easily – and the designs will be uniquely yours. The sunwheel motif used here is an ancient symbol with real energy. The colours chosen create a vibrant display that is best complemented by bright, attractive pot plants. Change the plants according to the season or to suit your mood. Three stamps, three colours of paint and a roll of masking tape are all you need to turn plain flowerpots into a sensational display.

You will need

- pencil
- tracing paper
- fine-tipped pen
- craft knife
- spray adhesive
- high-density foam, such as upholstery foam
- acrylic enamel paint in navy blue, red and cream
- plates
- glazed and plain terracotta flowerpots
- masking tape

1 Trace, transfer and cut out the pattern shapes from the template section. Lightly spray the shapes with adhesive and place them on the foam.

2 Use a craft knife to cut around the outlines of the large sunwheel motif. Scoop out the background and the pattern details.

3 Cut out the small motif, then scoop out the centre circle in the same way as the large sunwheel motif.

4 Spread an even coating of navy blue acrylic enamel paint on to a plate and press the large sunwheel motif into it. Make a test print to make sure that the stamp is not overloaded.

5 Stamp the large motif around the flowerpot four times. If you are using a larger flowerpot, you will be able to fit in more prints.

6 Spread an even coating of red acrylic enamel paint on to a plate and press the small motif into it. Make a test print to make sure the stamp is not overloaded. Stamp the small motif in groups above and below the large ones.

7 Cut out a small stepped triangle from foam using a craft knife.

8 Place two parallel strips of masking tape around the top end of a blue-glazed flowerpot. Leave a 1cm/½in gap between the two strips.

9 Squeeze some cream acrylic enamel paint on to a plate. With an offcut of foam, apply the paint to the gap between the two strips of masking tape.

10 Allow time for the paint to dry, then peel off the masking tape to reveal the cream border around the top of the pot.

11 Make sure the cream paint is spread evenly on a plate. Press the stepped triangle shape into it. Make a test print first, then stamp the pattern above and below the cream line, matching up the points of the triangle.

RIGHT: Make a mix-and-match set of stamped flowerpots, using coloured glazed pots or plain terracotta ones. One of these flowerpots, planted with spring flowers or bulbs, would make a lovely home-made gift.

DECORATED TILES

These days you can buy wonderful decorated tiles in all shapes and sizes, but they cost a fortune! So, why not use stamps and paint to make your own set of exclusive decorated tiles? Acrylic enamel paint resembles ordinary enamel, but it is in fact water-based and does not include harmful solvents. If you are decorating loose tiles, bake them in a domestic oven following the manufacturer's instructions to "fire" the colour and give added strength and permanence. The fired tiles will be waterproof and resilient to non-abrasive cleaning. If you are stamping on to a tiled wall, it is best to position the design where it will not need too much cleaning – the paint will certainly withstand an occasional soaking and can be wiped with a damp cloth.

You will need

- plain off-white tiles
- detergent and clean cloth
- acrylic enamel paint in blue and green
- plates
- foam rollers
- small, large and trellis heart stamps

1 Wash the tiles with detergent and hot water, then dry them thoroughly with a clean cloth before you apply any paint. The tiles must be clean and grease-free.

2 Spread some blue paint on to the plate and run a roller through it until it is evenly coated. Ink the small heart stamp and print two hearts side by side at the top of the tile, with equal spacing on either side.

3 Align the next two stamps directly below the first. Take care not to smudge the first two when stamping the second row. Acrylic enamel paint dries fast, so you only need to wait a few minutes to avoid smudges.

4 To make another design, ink the large heart stamp and make a single print on another off-white tile. Press the stamp down, then lift it off immediately to get an interesting surface texture.

5 Ink the large heart stamp and print overlapping the edges, so that the point is at the top edge of the tile and the curved part is at the bottom.

6 Ink the large heart stamp and make a first print with the heart angled to the left. Leave it to dry, then print another heart angled to the right as shown.

7 Spread some green paint on to a plate and run a roller through it until it is evenly coated. Ink the trellis heart stamp and print a single heart in the centre of a tile.

8 Continue printing a single trellis heart in the centre of each tile. The texture will be different on every print, making the tiles look far more interesting and giving an expensive hand-painted effect.

RIGHT: If you prefer, stamp less tiles with the heart motifs and use them as individual highlights on a chequerboard pattern of plain tiles. See the Country Kitchen project for an example of how to position the stamped tiles.

COUNTRY KITCHEN

Specialist suppliers sell beautifully decorated tiles but they can be very expensive. So why not use stamps and paint to make your own set of exclusive tiles? The grape stamp is inked with two shades of green that blend in the middle in a slightly different way each time. Small touches such as the rustic hanging rail and the wooden plate add rustic authenticity to a country kitchen. The wood for the rail needs to be old and weathered. The nails banged into the rail as hangers are called "cut" nails, which are used for floorboarding. Attach the rail to the wall and hang fresh herbs from it, conveniently close to the cooker (stove). The wooden plate is stamped with different parts of the tendril motif to make a decorative border and central design.

You will need

- plain tiles
- detergent and clean cloths
- acrylic enamel paint in blue-green and yellow-green
- plates
- foam rollers
- grape, leaf and tendril stamps
- emulsion (latex) or acrylic paint in olive-green
- scrap paper
- weathered piece of wood, maximum 30cm/12in long
- long "cut" nails or hooks
- hammer or drill
- black stamp pad
- scissors
- wooden plate, sanded to remove any stain or varnish
- vegetable oil

1 Wash the tiles in hot water and detergent, then wipe dry to ensure that there is no grease on the surface.

2 Spread some blue-green acrylic enamel paint on to one plate and some yellow-green paint on to another. Run the rollers through the paint until they are evenly coated.

3 Ink the leaf stamp and the top and right side of the grape stamp with the blue-green roller. Ink the rest of the grape stamp with the yellow-green roller.

4 Stamp a bunch of grapes in the centre of each tile. Remove the stamp directly, taking care not to smudge the print. If you do make a mistake, you can simply wipe off the paint with a clean cloth and start again. Follow the manufacturer's instructions to "fire" the tiles in the oven if required.

5 For the hanging rail, spread some olive-green emulsion (latex) or acrylic paint on to a plate and run a roller through it until it is evenly coated. Ink the leaf stamp and stamp twice on to scrap paper to remove some of the paint.

6 Stamp on to the length of weathered wood without re-inking the stamp. The resulting print will be light and faded-looking, like the wood itself. Make as many prints as you can fit along the length. Hammer in the nails or drill and screw in the hooks to complete the hanging rail.

7 For the wooden plate, stamp several tendrils on to scrap paper using the black stamp pad and cut them out. Arrange them on the plate to work out the spacing and positioning of the motifs.

8 Spread some olive-green emulsion or acrylic paint on to a plate and run a roller through it until it is evenly coated. Ink the corner of the tendril stamp comprising the two curls that will make up the border pattern. Carefully begin stamping these motifs around the edge of the plate.

9 Ink the whole stamp and stamp two tendrils in the centre of the plate. Leave the paint to dry.

10 Dip a clean cloth into some vegetable oil and rub this into the whole surface of the plate, including the stamped pattern. You can repeat this process once all the oil has been absorbed into the wood. Each time you rub oil into the plate, the colour of the wood will deepen.

RIGHT: Stamp co-ordinating motifs on tiles and wooden accessories, using different paints and techniques appropriate to each surface. Position the grape tiles as highlights or create an all-over effect, as illustrated in the Decorated Tiles project.

100% ALL NATURAL

STARRY VASE

The transparency of glass gives a new dimension to the stamped stars. The colour is applied to one surface, but the design is visible from all sides. You could try the stamps on any plain glass vase – this one was particularly easy to work with because of the flat surfaces. There are now some paints available called acrylic enamels. These are suitable for use on glass and ceramics and they give a hard-wearing finish that stands up to non-abrasive washing. The selection of colours is great, so take a look at them and try some glass stamping.

You will need

- glass vase
- detergent and clean cloth
- dark-coloured acrylic enamel paint
- plate
- foam roller
- large star stamp
- piece of glass

1 Wash the vase to remove any grease from the surface. Dry it thoroughly.

2 Spread some paint on to the plate and run the roller through it until it is evenly coated. Ink the stamp and make a test print on a piece of glass.

3 Stamp the stars randomly on to the glass vase. Apply gentle pressure with a steady hand and remove the stamp directly to avoid it sliding on the slippery surface.

FOLIAGE VASE

These stamped leaves will definitely add a designer touch to a plain glass vase, making it worthy of display with or without flowers or an arrangement of decorative leaves. The transparent glass allows the print to be seen from all sides, and the paint disperses on the smooth surface, adding texture to the leaves. Acrylic enamel paints are suitable for both glass and ceramics, and they have a consistency which works well with stamps. They also leave a glossy, hard-wearing finish that can be strengthened in an oven, if the manufacturer's instructions are followed carefully.

You will need

- plain rectangular glass vase
- detergent and clean cloth
- acrylic enamel paints in black and white
- plates
- foam rubber rollers
- leaf stamp

1 Wash the vase and wipe it dry with a clean cloth to ensure that there is no grease on the surface. Spread some black and white paint on to two plates. Run a roller through the white paint, and use it to ink the leaf stamp.

2 Print the first stamp on to the top half of the vase. Remove the stamp directly, taking care that it does not slide on the surface and smudge the print. If you make mistakes, they can be wiped off with a clean cloth.

3 Clean the leaf stamp and ink it with the black paint in the same way as with the white paint. Stamp a black leaf below the white one, so that it faces in the opposite direction. Allow to dry. If you wish to strengthen the paint in the oven, do so following the paint manufacturer's instructions.

HEARTS VASE

Take a plain vase and stamp it with rows of primary-coloured hearts to create a bright and cheerful display piece. Instead of being purely functional, the vase becomes artistic and decorative – this is one to put on the mantlepiece with or without cut flowers. There are now some paints available called acrylic enamels. These are suitable for use on glass and ceramics and they give a hard-wearing finish that stands up to non-abrasive washing. The selection of colours is great, so choose your own combination to suit the decor of your room.

You will need

- plain rectangular glass vase
- detergent and clean cloth
- acrylic enamel paints in yellow, blue and red
- plate
- foam roller
- small heart stamp

1 Wash the vase to remove any grease from the surface and dry it thoroughly. This will give you a better surface for stamping and will ensure a more successful print.

2 Spread a small amount of yellow paint on to the plate and run the roller through it until it is evenly coated. Ink the stamp and print a diagonal row of hearts on to the glass, starting at the top left-hand corner. Lift the stamp directly so that the prints are crisp and do not smudge.

3 Clean the stamp and ink it with blue paint. Add blue hearts in between the yellow ones as shown.

4 Clean the stamp and ink it with red paint. Then complete the design by adding the red hearts in the spaces left on the vase.

RIGHT: Repeating a simple motif in bright primary colours creates a very modern cheerful effect.

VALENTINE VASE

Present a dozen red roses in this beautiful stamped vase and you won't need Cupid's arrow to get your point across! There are a number of different types of glass paint on the market, but this vase is stamped with acrylic enamels, which work on glazed ceramics as well. The cupid is first stamped in cream, then painted over with a mottled white, achieved by dabbing paint on with a brush. A heart stencil is cut from card (stock) and used in combination with the cherub to complete the romantic valentine theme.

You will need

- pencil
- stencil card (stock) or plastic
- craft knife
- self-healing cutting mat
- plain rectangular glass vase
- acrylic enamel paint in red, cream and white
- plate
- foam roller
- stencil brush (optional)
- cherub stamp
- artist's paintbrush

1 Draw a heart shape on to a small piece of stencil card (stock) or plastic. Cut out the stencil with a craft knife on a self-healing cutting mat.

2 Position the heart stencil on the vase. Use red acrylic enamel paint and either the foam roller or the stencil brush to stencil the heart.

3 Spread some cream acrylic enamel paint on to a plate and run the roller through it until it is evenly coated. Ink the cherub stamp and make a print above the heart. Remove the stamp directly to prevent it from sliding. Use the artist's paintbrush to stipple a mottled coating of white paint over the cherub. Do not cover the whole print.

BLACK ROSE VASE

The transparency of this plain glass vase creates the illusion that the black rose is floating in mid-air, somewhere above the mantlepiece. Glass is an interesting surface to stamp on because it is so smooth that the paint disperses as soon as it is applied. It is a good idea to have a spare piece of glass handy so that you can practise your stamp before committing yourself to the final print. This way, you can find out how much paint you need to get the desired effect.

You will need

- glass vase
- detergent and clean cloth
- acrylic enamel paint in black
- plate
- foam roller
- large rose stamp
- piece of glass

1 Wash the vase to remove any grease from the surface, then dry it thoroughly with a clean cloth.

2 Spread some black paint on to the plate and run the roller through it until it is evenly coated. Ink the stamp and make a test print on the glass.

3 Stamp the black rose in the centre of the vase front. Apply gentle pressure with a steady hand and remove the stamp directly to avoid it sliding on the slippery surface. If you are not happy with the print, you can wipe it off before it begins to dry, clean the glass with a cloth and try again.

JAPANESE-STYLE VASE

Transform a plain glass vase with some chic calligraphic stamping. For this project, high-density foam was cut into strips, then dipped into acrylic enamel paint. The strips were then twisted into different shapes to make a series of quick prints. Don't make too many prints – the end result should look like an enlargement of a Japanese calligraphic symbol. The paint finish is tough enough to withstand gentle washing, but take care, because all unfired surface decoration such as this is prone to chipping and peeling.

You will need

- set square (triangle)
- felt-tipped pen
- high-density foam, such as upholstery foam, 25 x 10 x 5cm/10 x 4 x 2in
- craft knife
- plain rectangular glass vase
- detergent and clean cloth
- acrylic enamel paint in black
- plate

1 Using a set square and felt-tipped pen, draw lines 1cm/½in apart along the length of the foam.

2 Cut along the lines using a craft knife, then part the foam and cut all the way through it.

3 Clean the vase thoroughly with a clean cloth to remove any surface grease and dry it well.

4 Spread an even coating of paint on to a plate. Curl up a strip of foam and dip it into the paint.

5 Use both hands, positioned just above the glass surface, to curl the foam strip into an open-ended shape. When the curve looks right, press it on to the vase. Lift it off straight away to avoid any smudging.

6 Press a straight strip of foam into the paint, then use it to continue the line around the side of the vase.

7 Complete the calligraphic design with a series of these straight black lines. Use different width strips of foam if necessary. Applying the pressure unevenly will give a more authentic effect.

RIGHT: Simple strips and curls of foam make very effective stamps. They can also be used on a curved glass surface.

SNOWFLAKE STORAGE JARS

Almost every kitchen could do with the occasional facelift. Rather than pay for a completely new look, why not just cheer up your storage jars and give your kitchen a breath of fresh air? You can create a whole new atmosphere by stamping patterns on your jars with acrylic enamel paint. The finish is quite tough and will stand up to occasional gentle washing, but will not withstand the dishwasher. Choose a design that suits your kitchen, or copy the pattern for the motif used here.

You will need

- pencil
- tracing paper
- spray adhesive
- high-density foam, such as upholstery foam
- craft knife
- detergent and clean cloth
- glass storage jars
- acrylic enamel paint in white
- plate
- tile

1 Trace and transfer the pattern shape from the template section. Lightly spray the shape with adhesive and place it on the foam. Cut around the outline with a craft knife.

2 Cut horizontally into the foam to meet the outline cuts then remove the excess foam.

3 Clean the glass jars thoroughly with detergent and a cloth, then dry them well. This will remove any grease and will provide a better surface.

4 Spread an even coating of paint on to the plate. Press the stamp into it and make a test print on a tile to make sure that the stamp is not overloaded.

5 Holding the jar steady with your spare hand, press the foam stamp around the side of the jar.

6 Rotate the stamp 90 degrees and make a second print directly below the first. Continue in this way, alternating the angle of the stamp with each print. Cover the whole surface of the jar with the snowflake motifs.

RIGHT: A flexible foam stamp is ideal for printing on a rounded glass surface. Experiment with other simple shapes.

VINTAGE GLASS BOWL

Turn a plain glass bowl into an exquisite table centrepiece by stamping a white tendril pattern on the outside. Stamped glassware looks wonderful because the opaque pattern seems to intermingle as you look through the transparent glass. Another advantage is that you can see the stamp as the print is being made, which helps you to position it correctly and avoid overlaps and smudges. Glass painting has become popular recently and there are several brands of specialist glass paint available. Acrylic enamel paint has a good consistency for stamping and is water-based, allowing you to simply wipe it off and start again if you make a mistake.

You will need

- plain glass bowl
- detergent and clean cloth
- acrylic enamel paint in white
- plate
- foam roller
- tendril stamp

1 Wash the bowl in hot water and detergent, then wipe dry to ensure that there is no grease on the surface. Spread some white acrylic enamel paint on to the plate and run the roller through it until it is evenly coated.

2 Ink the tendril stamp and stamp the first row of prints around the base of the bowl. Remove the stamp directly, taking care that it does not slide or smudge the print. If you do make a mistake, wipe off the paint with a clean cloth and start again.

3 Turn the stamp the other way up to stamp the second row of motifs. Position the prints in between the tendrils on the first row, so that there are no obvious gaps in the design.

4 Stamp one more row with the stamp the original way up. Allow the stamp to overlap the edge of the bowl, so that most of the stem is left out. Leave the bowl to dry or "fire" it in the oven to fix the design, following the paint manufacturer's instructions.

BELOW: The delicate tendril design would also look attractive in a pale shade of green for a more modern effect.

ACCESSORIES

Accessories are probably the ideal starting-point if you have never considered a rubber stamp as a decorating tool. You can transform a lampshade, picture frame or wooden tray in minutes, with minimal effort and even less mess. All you need is a stamp and an inkpad to create an all-over pattern, then a quick rinse with water to clean the stamp. What could be easier? Starting a new craft activity is often the most difficult part, so it makes sense to begin with something small, until you have built up the confidence to attempt more ambitious projects. This shouldn't take long, because stamping is so easy and so little can go wrong.

ABOVE: A wide range of accessories are suitable for stamping, for example giftwrap, book covers, lampshades, as well as this cutlery rack.

LEFT: Most of the projects in this section use ready-made stamps. Printing on paper is particularly simple and inexpensive.

GLORIOUS GIFTWRAP

If you want to make a gift extra special, why not print your own wrapping paper, designed to suit the person to whom you are giving the present? All you need is a selection of rubber stamps, inkpads or paint, and plain paper. Your home-made giftwrap will show that you really wanted to make the gift memorable. Stamped paper is great at Christmas when you need to wrap lots of presents at the same time. Your gifts will look very individual, particularly if you continue the motif on to the labels.

You will need

- plain paper
- rubber stamps in a variety of motifs
- stamp inkpads

1 To make a non-regimented design, like this clover-leaf pattern, first stamp at one edge of the paper. Then rotate the stamp in your hand to change the direction of each print. Continue stamping the design, judging the spacing by eye and printing the motifs close together. Re-charge the stamp with ink as required.

2 Turn the paper and continue stamping the shapes. The end result should have roughly an even amount of background to pattern.

3 To achieve a more formal pattern, like this bird design, begin by stamping a row of shapes along the bottom edge.

4 Build up the design, alternating between two colours if you like, as shown here, to make an all-over pattern of closely spaced shapes.

RIGHT: Experiment with different motifs, repeating them to make all-over patterns. Try different kinds of paper, for example brown parcel wrap or tissue paper.

STARRY WRAPPING PAPER

Here is a way to print your own wrapping paper that will look better than any paper available in the High Street. The design will be unique and it hardly costs anything at all, unlike the hand-printed top-of-the-range designs available commercially. People have always enjoyed the satisfying activity of making repeat patterns, and nowadays we only really get a chance to do so at nursery school. But now you can grab some sheets of plain paper or colourful tissue paper, clear the kitchen table and start stamping lots of different patterns.

You will need

- ruler
- pencil
- brown parcel wrap
- acrylic paint in brown, blue, white and cream
- plate
- foam roller
- starburst, folk-art and small star stamps

1 Use the ruler and pencil to mark one edge of the brown parcel wrap at approximately 12cm/5in intervals.

2 Spread a small amount of brown paint on to the plate and run the roller through it until it is evenly coated. Ink the starburst stamp and print on to the parcel wrap, using the pencil marks as a guide for the first row and judging the next rows by eye.

3 Ink the folk-art stamp with blue paint and stamp these stars in the spaces between the brown stars.

ABOVE: Create your own designs using different star stamps. Use different colours for specific occasions, for example red and gold paints would be ideal for Christmas.

4 Ink the small star stamp with white paint and carefully fill in the centres of the blue stars.

5 Stamp cream stars along diagonal lines between the rows of blue and brown stars.

CHRISTENING PARTY

The giftwrap, cards and table setting of this project will all help to make a traditional christening or naming-day party an unforgettable occasion. Use the cherubs to announce the baby's birth and herald the start of the celebrations. Buy a good-quality white paper for the cards. Some papers are deckle-edged, while others are textured. The choice is a personal one and a textured surface will give interesting stamped effects, so experiment on samples of paper. Set off the hand-printed wrapping paper by tying the parcels with white satin ribbons and bows.

You will need

- large white tablecloth or sheet
- backing card (stock)
- 1 swag and 2 cherub stamps
- fabric paint in bottle-green and silver
- plates
- foam rollers
- iron
- paper table napkins in white and bottle-green
- acrylic paint in bottle-green, white and blue-grey
- white notepaper
- scissors
- ruler
- pencil
- water-based size
- silver transfer leaf
- soft cloth
- fine wire (steel) wool
- silver wrapping paper
- newspaper
- black stamp pad
- scrap paper
- small strip of card

1 Lay the tablecloth or sheet on to the backing card (stock). Ink the swag stamp with bottle-green fabric paint and print across one corner of the cloth, so that the tassels are about 2.5cm/1in from the edges. Stamp swags all around the edge of the cloth to create a scalloped effect.

2 Spread some silver fabric paint on to a plate and run a roller through it until it is evenly coated. Ink both cherub stamps and, alternating the two designs, make a print above every other swag all round the edge of the cloth.

3 Continue to stamp a widely spaced cherub pattern in the centre of the cloth, alternating both stamps and rotating the direction of the prints. Follow the manufacturer's instructions to fix (set) the fabric paint with an iron.

4 For the napkins, spread some bottle-green acrylic paint on to a plate and run a roller through it until it is evenly coated. Ink the cherub stamps and make one print on each white table napkin.

5 Spread some white acrylic paint on to a plate. Use a roller to ink the cherub stamps. Stamp a white cherub on each green napkin.

6 To make the cards, cut and fold the paper to the required size, at least 14 x 11.5cm/5½ x 4½in. Draw pencil lines on the back of the stamp block to mark the mid-points on each side to help position the stamp accurately. Spread some blue-grey acrylic paint on to a plate and run a roller through it until it is evenly coated. Ink the stamp and print cherubs on the cards. Leave to dry.

7 Spread water-based size on to a plate and run a roller through it until it is evenly coated. Ink the cherub stamps with size and overprint the blue-grey prints. Leave to dry for the time recommended by the manufacturer until the size becomes tacky. Lay sheets of silver leaf on to the size and burnish the backing paper with a soft cloth.

8 Remove the backing paper and use wire (steel) wool to rub away excess silver leaf still clinging to the paper.

9 To make the wrapping paper, lay the silver paper on some newspaper on a flat surface. Using the black stamp pad, stamp several cherubs and swags on scrap paper and cut them out. Arrange the paper motifs on the silver paper to plan your design. Cut a card strip as a guide to the spacing between the motifs.

10 Spread some bottle-green acrylic paint on to a plate and run a roller through it until it is evenly coated. Ink the cherub stamp and print cherubs on the silver paper. Use the card strip to space the stamps.

11 Ink the swag stamp with white acrylic paint and print the linking swags between the cherub motifs.

RIGHT: Your guests will be delighted with hand-printed co-ordinating invitations and table linen for a special occasion such as a christening, wedding or silver wedding. For a golden wedding party, use gold fabric paint and gold wrapping paper.

BOHEMIAN BOOK COVERS

Brown parcel wrap is perfect book-covering material – it is strong, folds crisply and costs very little. The paper usually has a shiny side and a matt side, with the matt side more absorbent to paint. Pattern making with potato cuts is great fun, and the elements used here – a small solid square, a square outline, and a triangle – can be used in different combinations to make a variety of designs. Use the three paint colours to make your own design. These papers would make ideal covers for a row of cookbooks on a kitchen shelf. The watercolour paint is mixed with PVA (white) glue which dries transparent, leaving a slight sheen that looks great combined with the characteristic potato-cut texture.

You will need

- knife
- 2 potatoes
- bowl
- PVA (white) glue
- paintbrush
- watercolour paint in brick-red, brown and yellow-ochre
- plate
- craft knife
- brown parcel wrap

1 Cut the potatoes in half with a knife, then trim the edges to give them all the same square shape.

2 In a bowl mix PVA (white) glue and water in equal amounts, then add a drop of watercolour paint. The texture should be thick and sticky.

3 Spread an even coating of the paint mixture on to a plate then dip a potato into it – this will make it easier to see the design as you cut it out. Leave a square border around the edge of the potato shape, then divide the rest of the surface diagonally. Scoop out one triangular section with a craft knife.

4 Print a row of this pattern along the bottom edge of the paper.

RIGHT: A humble potato cut can be repeated to build up sophisticated geometric designs and create a co-ordinating set of book covers.

5 Stamp the following row with the same stamp the other way up. Add variety to the design by rotating the stamp for each new row, to form different patterns.

6 To make a chequerboard pattern, leave a gap between the prints. Dip a small piece of potato into the paint and stamp dots in the middle of the blank squares. Experiment with your own combinations.

WEDDING ALBUM COVER

Custom-made wedding photograph albums are never as special as one you make yourself. For most of us, a wedding is the only time we are photographed professionally looking our very best, so the presentation should do the pictures justice. The album should have a solid spine, so don't choose the spiral-bound type. Visit a specialist paper dealer and discover the wonderful range of textured papers. The paper is stamped with gold size and gold leaf is laid on to it to create gleaming golden cherubs and swags. Initials or the date of the wedding add the finishing touch.

You will need

- large photograph album with a solid spine
- white textured paper
- scissors or craft knife
- double-sided tape
- cherub and swag stamps
- black stamp pad
- scrap paper
- gold size
- plate
- foam roller
- gold transfer leaf
- soft-bristled paintbrush
- gold transfer letters or fine artist's brush (optional)

1 Lay the opened album on the sheet of paper and trim the paper to size. Allow a border round the edges to fold over the paper inside the cover. Cover the album with the paper, sticking down the overlaps on the inside of the cover.

2 Stamp several cherubs and swags on scrap paper and cut them out. Lay them out on the album cover with any initials or dates to plan your design. When you are happy with the design, use the paper cut-outs as a guide for positioning the stamps.

3 Spread some gold size on to the plate and run the roller through it until it is evenly coated. Ink the stamps with size and stamp the design on the album cover. Leave to dry for the time recommended by the manufacturer until the size becomes tacky.

4 Lay sheets of gold leaf on to the size and burnish with a soft brush.

5 Brush away any excess gold leaf still clinging to the paper. Add initials and the date, if required, using gold transfer letters or paint them freehand in size and gild as before.

BELOW: Gold leaf stamped on textured white paper is a beautiful way to remember a very special day.

STATIONERY, NOTEBOOKS AND FOLDERS

Have fun experimenting with stamp designs and create your own range of stationery at the same time. The stamps can be used alone or in combination with each other to make a whole range of patterns linked by the use of colour to form a set. Here, the plain books, folders and stationery are all a natural brown and the pattern is stamped in a sepia tone, which complements the colour of the paper. Mixing extender or PVA (white) glue into the paint will make the paint dry more slowly, giving you extra time to work. Hand-printed stationery is very quick and easy to make and will give great pleasure for your own use or as an individual gift.

You will need

- sepia acrylic paint
- plates
- extender or PVA (white) glue
- foam rollers
- grape, tendril and leaf stamps
- scrap paper
- notebooks
- brown parcel wrap
- craft knife
- self-healing cutting mat
- acrylic or emulsion (latex) paint in off-white
- folder
- square-tipped artist's paintbrush
- small file
- handmade paper folded into cards
- natural brown envelopes

1 Spread some sepia acrylic paint on to a plate. Add extender or PVA (white) glue and mix together.

2 Run a roller through the paint until it is evenly coated and ink the grape stamp. Make several test prints on scrap paper to gauge the way the paper absorbs the paint and how much paint you will need to apply to the stamp to achieve the desired effect.

3 Stamp the first bunch of grapes in the middle of one of the notebook covers.

4 Ink the tendril stamp and surround the grapes with tendril motifs. The pattern can be repeated on the back cover of the notebook.

5 Stamp a bunch of grapes on to a small piece of brown parcel wrap. Carefully cut around the outline with a craft knife on a self-healing cutting mat to make a stencil.

6 Spread some off-white paint on to a plate and run a roller through it until it is evenly coated. Position the stencil on a notebook cover and run the roller over the stencil to make a solid grape shape. Leave to dry.

7 Ink the grape stamp with sepia acrylic paint and overprint the stencilled shape to add the detail.

8 For the folder, cut a window out of a sheet of scrap paper the same size as the folder cover to make a paper frame.

9 Lay the window frame on the cover. Ink the leaf stamp with sepia paint and stamp leaves all over the cover, overlapping the frame. Leave to dry, then remove the frame to reveal a plain border around the leaf pattern.

10 Mix some off-white paint into the sepia to make a lighter brown. Using a brush, apply the lighter brown paint to one side of the grape stamp and sepia to the other.

11 Stamp a single bunch of grapes on to the cover of a small file. The bunch of grapes will be shaded on one side, creating an interesting three-dimensional effect.

12 Place the folded cards of handmade paper on sheets of scrap paper. Stamp an all-over pattern of sepia tendrils, overlapping the edges so that the cards look as if they have been cut from a larger sheet of stamped paper. The texture of the paper will show through in places and the colour will vary as the paint gradually wears off the stamp, adding to the rich, handmade effect.

RIGHT: Once you realize how easy it is to make stamped stationery, notebooks and folders, there will be no turning back. For example, you could also print the grape stamp at the top of sheets of notepaper.

HERALDIC STATIONERY

Design and print a personalized set of stationery to add a touch of elegance to all your correspondence. Heraldic motifs have been used for centuries to decorate letters and secret diaries, but it is no longer necessary to live in a palace to be able to use them. This project demonstrates the variety of ways in which a single stamp can be used to produce different effects. The resulting stationery is based on a common theme but with plenty of individual flourishes. Experiment with your favourite colour combinations and try all-over or border patterns to add even more variety. Many craft shops sell special embossing powders that can be heated to produce a raised print.

You will need

- dark blue artist's watercolour paint
- plates
- foam rollers
- diamond, fleur-de-lys and crown stamps
- brown parcel wrap
- craft knife
- self-healing cutting mat
- small notebook, folder, postcards and textured and plain white notepaper
- gold paint
- dark blue paper
- ruler
- set square (triangle)
- paper glue
- fine artist's paintbrush

1 Spread some dark blue watercolour paint on to a plate and run a roller through it until it is evenly coated. Ink the diamond stamp and print one motif on to a small piece of the brown parcel wrap.

2 Cut out the diamond shape with a craft knife on a self-healing cutting mat. Try not to over-cut the corners because the shape will be used as a stencil and the paint may bleed through.

3 Position the paper stencil in the middle of the notebook cover and use the roller to apply dark blue watercolour paint through it. Leave to dry.

4 Spread some gold paint on to a plate and run the roller through it until it is evenly coated. Ink the diamond stamp and stamp a gold print directly over the solid blue diamond, lining up the edges as closely as possible.

5 Cut a rectangle the size of the fleur-de-lys stamp block out of dark blue paper. Measure and divide it in half lengthways. Cut away one side with a craft knife, leaving a narrow border around the edge to make a window in one side.

6 Using a ruler and set square (triangle) to position the stamp, print a dark blue fleur-de-lys in the centre of the folder. Glue the blue paper over the print so that half the fleur-de-lys motif shows through the window.

7 Ink the fleur-de-lys stamp with gold paint. Cover the cut-out side of the design with a straight-edged piece of parcel wrap. Stamp a gold fleur-de-lys to align with the sides of the blue print. Remove the piece of parcel wrap to reveal the final design, which will be half gold and half blue.

8 Stamp a blue fleur-de-lys on a notebook cover or postcard. Cover one half of it with a straight-edged piece of parcel wrap and overprint in gold to make a two-colour print.

9 Fold a piece of textured notepaper to make a card. Stamp a blue fleur-de-lys on the front of the card. The texture of the paper will show through in places. Add flourishes of gold paint using a fine artist's paintbrush.

10 Stamp a gold crown at the top of textured and plain white sheets of notepaper.

RIGHT: Experiment with other stamps and colours to create your own personalized stationery.

BOOK COVERS AND SECRETS BOX

This project evokes another era, when time passed by more slowly and leisure had nothing to do with aerobic exercise. Diaries and scrapbooks were kept and lovingly covered with printed papers and secret mementoes were hidden in locked wooden caskets. Recapture the spirit of a bygone age by stamping patterned papers and using them to bind sketchbooks, albums and diaries. Preserve the battered antiquity of an old wooden box by stamping it and lining it in muted shades of red and green, then rubbing back the paint to simulate years of wear and tear.

You will need

- black ink stamp pad
- tulip, leaf and pineapple stamps
- scrap paper
- scissors
- sugar (construction) paper
- ready-mixed watercolour paint in a droppered bottle in deep red, leaf-green and black
- plates
- long ruler
- diary, photo album or book, such as a sketchbook
- PVA (white) glue
- black bookbinding tape
- self-healing cutting mat
- craft knife
- old wooden box
- emulsion (latex) or acrylic paint in brick-red and sage-green
- foam roller
- wooden batten (furring strip)
- lining brush
- fine-grade abrasive paper (sandpaper) or wire (steel) wool
- furniture polish and soft cloth (optional)

1 For the book cover, use the stamp pad to print four tulips on scrap paper. Cut them out and arrange them in a row along the top edge of the sugar (construction) paper, side by side and alternately facing up and down. Use these paper prints as a guide for stamping.

2 Spread some deep red watercolour paint on to a plate and dip the stamp into it. Lay the ruler across the paper and use to align the stamp to print the first row. Re-ink the stamp after three prints for an irregular hand-printed effect.

3 Move the ruler down the width of a stamp block for each new row. Stamp the rows so that the tulips lie between the prints in the previous row. Cover the paper completely and leave to dry. Print more sugar paper, using the leaf and pineapple stamps and the leaf-green and black paint.

4 Cover the books with the stamped paper, sticking down any mitred corners with PVA (white) glue. Place a strip of bookbinding tape along the spine to cover the paper edges so there is an equal width of tape on the front and back cover. Trim away the tape at the top and bottom with a craft knife.

5 For the secrets box, use the stamp pad to print some tulips and leaves on scrap paper and cut them out. Arrange them on the wooden box to plan your design, deciding which motifs will be red and which green.

6 Spread some brick-red emulsion (latex) or acrylic paint on to a plate and run the roller through it until it is evenly coated. Ink the stamps and remove one paper shape at a time to stamp a leaf or tulip motif in its place.

7 Ink the leaf stamp with sage-green paint and stamp green leaves on the secrets box in the same way.

8 Place the wooden batten (furring strip) along the edge of the box and use the sage-green paint and the lining brush to paint an outline around the box and corner motifs. Slide your hand along the batten to keep an even line.

9 Leave the paint to dry completely, then lightly distress the stamped prints with abrasive paper (sandpaper) or wire (steel) wool. The secrets box can then be polished with furniture polish, if desired.

RIGHT: Sugar paper makes an effective background to the "distressed", aged stamp designs and is the ideal weight for book covers. If sugar paper is not readily available, you could use brown parcel wrap.

TREASURE BOXES

Sets of lidded round boxes made from lightweight wood, card (stock) or papier-mâché are often imported from the Far East and are readily available in the stores. The plain ones, sometimes called blanks, are not expensive and they make the ideal base for some imaginative stamping work. The hearts in this project have been grouped to form a larger motif, with some of them only partially stamped, so they don't look like hearts. As you can see, experimentation produces all sorts of variations on the heart theme.

You will need

- set of plain, round boxes with lids
- emulsion (latex) or acrylic paint in light grey, orange and black
- paintbrush
- plate
- foam roller
- large and small heart stamps

1 Paint the lid of the box light grey with emulsion (latex) or acrylic paint. Leave to dry. If extra coverage is needed, apply more than one coat, leaving to dry between coats.

2 Spread some orange paint on to the plate and run the roller through it until it is evenly coated. Then ink the large heart stamp. Print the top half of the hearts around the side of the lid. Do not print the hearts too closely together – use the stamp to estimate the spacing before you begin.

3 Align the stamp with the pattern printed on the side of the lid, then print the pointed part of each heart around the top of the lid. This gives the impression that the hearts have been folded over the lid.

4 Use the same pointed part of the heart to print a zigzag border around the bottom edge of the box.

5 Still using the orange paint, stamp one complete large heart in the centre of the lid. Ink the small stamp with black paint and stamp a circle of hearts with their points radiating outwards between the yellow "V" shapes.

BELOW: It is amazing how many different patterns can be created using a couple of simple motifs.

MATISSE PICTURE FRAME

You can create instant art by combining stamp leaf prints with blocks of bright colour on a picture frame. Matisse's stunning cut-outs were the inspiration for this project. In his later life, Matisse used paper cuttings to create collage pictures that are as bold and fresh today as when they were first made. For the framed image, print a single leaf on to paper and enlarge it on a photocopier. Print it on to coloured paper and make a simple cut-out.

You will need

- broad wooden picture frame
- emulsion (latex) paint in black
- paintbrush
- set square (triangle)
- pencil
- artist's acrylic, gouache or poster paints in lime-green and fuchsia
- plate
- foam roller
- leaf stamp
- clear matt (flat) varnish and brush

1 Paint the frame in black (latex) emulsion and let it dry. Use a set square (triangle) and pencil to mark four squares in the corners of the frame, with sides the same as the width of the wood.

2 Paint the corner squares lime-green. You will need to apply several coats of paint for the most intense colour. Make sure that none of the black background shows through the lime-green.

3 Spread some fuchsia paint on to a plate and run the roller through it until it is evenly coated. Ink the leaf stamp and stamp one leaf in each lime-green corner. Rotate the stamp each time, so that the stem of the leaf always points inwards.

ABOVE: This work of art is surprisingly easy to achieve. Matisse's cut-outs will give you other ideas for colour schemes.

4 Let the paint dry, then apply a coat of clear matt (flat) varnish to seal and protect the picture frame.

STARRY PICTURE FRAME

This project combines many of the creative possibilities of stamping. It involves four processes: painting a background, stamping in one colour, overprinting in a second colour and rubbing back to the wood. These processes transform a plain wooden frame and they are neither time-consuming nor expensive. It is surprisingly difficult to find small, old frames that are broad enough to stamp. Fortunately, a wide range of basic, cheap frames can be found in do-it-yourself stores.

You will need

- picture frame
- emulsion (latex) paint in sky-blue, red-brown and gold
- paintbrush
- plate
- foam roller
- small and large star stamps
- fine wire (steel) wool or abrasive paper (sandpaper)

1 Paint the picture frame with sky-blue emulsion (latex) paint and leave it to dry thoroughly.

2 Spread a small amount of red-brown paint on to the plate and run the roller through it until it is evenly coated. Ink the small star stamp and print it in the middle of each side.

3 Using the red-brown paint, stamp a large star over each corner of the frame. Leave to dry thoroughly.

4 Ink the large stamp with gold paint and overprint the red-brown corner stars. Leave to dry before rubbing the frame gently with wire (steel) wool or abrasive paper (sandpaper) to give it a slightly aged appearance.

BELOW: *Experiment with other stamps, choosing one to suit the frame. Large stars overlap the sides of this deep frame.*

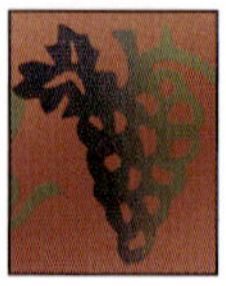

GRAPE PICTURE FRAME

A decorated frame draws attention to the picture within, while providing another opportunity to add colour and pattern to a room. This frame can be hung with the broad end at either the top or the bottom, depending on the nature of the picture it surrounds. The balance of the grape, leaf and tendril motif is reinforced by using the same colours to paint the border lines. Practise using a long-bristled lining brush on paper first before you paint the fine lines on the frame. The "hands-on" style does not require perfection – slightly wavy lines add character.

You will need

- grape, leaf and tendril stamps
- black stamp pad
- scrap paper
- scissors
- picture frame, painted brick-red with an olive-green border
- set square (triangle)
- pencil
- emulsion (latex) or acrylic paint in olive-green and ultramarine blue
- plate
- foam roller
- long-bristled lining brush
- damp cloth (optional)

1 Stamp all three motifs on to scrap paper and cut them out. Position them on the broad end of the picture frame to plan your design.

2 Use a set square (triangle) and pencil to draw a line around the frame, just inside the green border. Draw a second line around the centre of the frame.

3 Spread some olive-green paint on to one side of the plate and blue on to the other. Run the roller through the paint until it is evenly coated, allowing the colours to blend slightly in the middle. Ink the stamps and print the motifs in the planned positions.

4 Use the lining brush to paint the pencil lines ultramarine blue. Steady your hand by sliding it along the raised border as you work. If you make a very obvious mistake, wipe off the paint immediately with a damp cloth, but you may need to touch up the background colour when the new line has dried.

RIGHT: Choose stamp motifs and a colour scheme to complement your favourite picture.

SEEDPOD LAMPSHADE

Unusual lampshades can be very expensive. The solution is to take a plain lampshade and apply some surface decoration that will transform it from a utility object into a stylish focal point. This design, which resembles a seedpod, is easy to cut from high-density foam. It makes a bold, sharp-edged print and the flexibility of the foam means that it can bend around the curved surface. Remember to extend the pattern beyond the edges of the lampshade, so that only parts of the motifs appear. The lampshade will look as if it has been made from hand-printed fabric.

You will need

- pencil
- tracing paper
- spray adhesive
- high-density foam, such as upholstery foam
- craft knife
- thinned emulsion (latex) paint in creamy yellow and pale blue
- plates
- small rubber roller
- plain-coloured lampshade

1 Trace and transfer the seedpod pattern shape from the template section. Lightly spray the shape with adhesive and place it on the foam. Cut out the motif using a craft knife. Cut around the outline first, going all the way through the foam. Cut around the centre detail to a depth of about 1cm/½in, then under-cut and scoop out this section, and cut away the background.

2 Spread some creamy yellow paint on to a plate and coat the roller evenly. Use it to apply a coating of paint to the stamp.

3 Make the first print a partial one, using only the top end of the stamp. Continue to print at random angles, leaving plenty of spaces for the second colour. Wash the stamp, removing all traces of yellow paint.

BELOW: The outline shape looks like a stencil, but it is in fact all part of the home-made foam stamp.

4 Spread some pale blue paint on a second plate and coat the roller. Use it to apply an even coating of paint to the stamp.

5 Stamp blue shapes at random angles in between the yellow ones. Be sure to make some partial prints so that the pattern continues over the edges.

FLORAL LAMPSHADE

A new lampshade can work wonders, freshening up a dull corner and providing as much in the way of style as in illumination. This paper shade has a good shape with interesting punched edges. However, a plain shade would work equally well for this project. In this design it is essential to space the rose pattern accurately, so make a quick paper pattern to ensure perfect results with every print.

You will need

- emulsion (latex) or fabric paint in pink and green
- plate
- 2 square-tipped paintbrushes
- large rose stamp
- scrap paper
- scissors
- masking tape
- plain lampshade (either paper or cloth)

1 Spread some pink and green paint on to the plate. Using the square-tipped paintbrushes, ink the leaves of the rose stamp green and the flower pink. (If one colour mixes with the other, just wipe them off and re-ink the stamp.)

2 Print five rose motifs on to scrap paper and cut them out.

3 Using masking tape, stick the paper roses round the lampshade. Make sure that they are spaced the same distance apart and not too close together. Depending on the size of the shade, you should be able to fit four or five roses round it.

4 Re-ink the stamp and lift off each paper rose individually as you stamp on to the lampshade itself. Hold the lampshade firmly with your spare hand and roll the stamp across the curved surface to get an even print.

RIGHT: This would be an ideal accessory for one of the rose fabric projects in this book.

STARFISH LAMP

This project transforms a plain, ordinary lamp into an individual and stylish accessory. Buy the cheapest lamp you can find because, once the base has been painted and the shade stamped, you won't be able to recognize the item you bought originally. The deep red stamps on the pink background not only give out a lovely coloured glow when the lamp is switched on, but cheer up a dull corner even when switched off.

You will need

- lamp with fabric shade and wooden base
- emulsion (latex) paint in deep red and light grey-blue
- paintbrush
- plates
- pencil
- foam roller
- starfish stamp

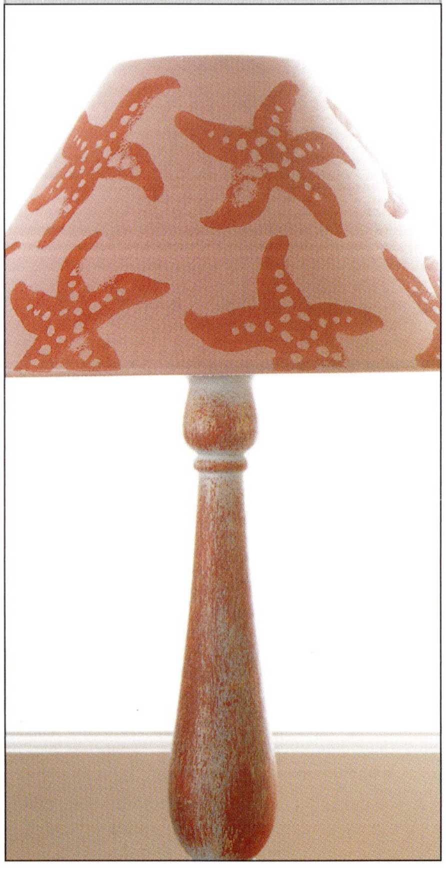

1 Paint the base of the lamp with deep red emulsion (latex) paint and leave to dry thoroughly.

2 Using a dry brush and a small amount of light grey-blue paint, lightly brush on the colour to shade the shape of the turned wood.

3 Use the stamp block to work out the spacing of the starfish round the shade. Lightly mark the design in pencil. Spread some deep red paint on to a plate and run the roller through it until it is evenly coated. Ink the stamp and begin by printing the bottom row of the pattern, following the pencil marks.

4 Stamp a row of starfish around the top of the shade. Remember to check the spacing as you go – you will fit fewer around the top than the bottom.

ABOVE: Simple stamping on the lampshade is given extra interest by painting and overpainting the base in two colours. Choose a colour scheme to suit your room.

FOLK COFFEE CANISTER

Rescue an old kitchen canister and give it a new identity as a piece of folk art. Painted tinware was very popular with early American settlers, and for years peddlers roamed the countryside loaded down with brightly painted cans, pitchers and bowls they sold from door to door. All these years later tinware is still a popular way of brightening up kitchen shelves. Prepare this canister by rubbing down the old paint with abrasive paper (sandpaper) to provide a surface for a fresh coat of emulsion (latex) paint. After stamping, bring out the colour and protect the surface with several coats of clear varnish.

You will need

- empty coffee canister
- abrasive paper (sandpaper)
- small household paintbrush
- emulsion (latex) paint in brick-red, black and bright red
- fine artist's paintbrushes
- plates
- foam roller
- tulip stamp
- clear gloss varnish and brush

1 Sand the canister. Paint the canister and lid brick-red. Leave to dry, then paint the rim of the lid black using a fine artist's paintbrush.

2 Run the roller through the black paint until it is evenly coated. Ink the tulip stamp and print a tulip on the side of the canister, tilting the stamp block around the curve of the canister.

3 Fill in the tulip shape carefully, using bright red paint and a fine artist's paintbrush.

ABOVE: *Stamping works well on tin surfaces. In this project, the tulip shape is filled in using a fine artist's paintbrush.*

4 Apply several coats of gloss varnish to seal and protect the canister. Allow each coat to dry completely before applying the next.

VINE LEAF CUTLERY RACK

A small wooden cutlery rack like this one provides another ideal surface for stamping. Use the stamps to loosely co-ordinate your kitchen or dining room without being swamped by matching patterns and colours. The wood has been stained blue and is then rubbed back to reveal some of the natural grain underneath. The two colours of the pattern are stamped separately using thinned emulsion (latex) paint for a light and airy finish.

You will need

- wooden cutlery rack, stained blue
- fine abrasive paper (sandpaper)
- emulsion (latex) or acrylic paint in dark and light olive-green
- plates
- foam roller
- leaf stamp

BELOW: This design would look very attractive stamped on the top of a pine shelf unit or kitchen dresser.

1 Sand the surface of the cutlery rack to reveal some of the grain. Spread some dark olive-green paint on to a plate and thin it with water until it is a runny consistency.

2 Use the roller to ink the leaf stamp. Print two leaves side by side on the back and front of the rack as shown. Print two leaves one above the other on the sides. Leave to dry.

3 Spread some light olive-green paint on to a plate and run the roller through it until it is evenly coated. Ink just the tips of the leaves and overprint all the darker green prints. If some of the prints are slightly off-register, this will only add to the rustic appearance of the cutlery rack.

CANDLE BOX

A long time ago every home would have had a candle box hanging on the kitchen wall, kept full to meet the lighting needs of the household. Although rarely needed in quite the same way today, candle boxes are still popular and add to a comfortable atmosphere. Candle boxes can be bought, but are quite easy to make from five pieces of wood. The open top allows you to see when your supply is running low and the sight of the new candles is somehow reassuring as well as attractive.

You will need

- wooden candle box
- fine-grade abrasive paper (sandpaper)
- shellac and brush
- dark oak woodstain
- plate
- foam roller
- diamond, crown and fleur-de-lys stamps
- lining brush

BELOW: This box has a heraldic theme.

1 Sand away any varnish and smooth any rough edges on the box.

2 Paint the bare wood with a single coat of shellac.

3 Spread some woodstain on to a plate and run the roller through it until it is evenly coated. Ink the stamps and print a single motif on each side of the box. Print the fleur-de-lys so it will be visible above the candles. Use the lining brush to paint a thin border on all sides of the box.

WOODEN WINE CRATE

Old wood usually looks best with a faded rather than freshly painted pattern. The grape design here does not detract from the crate's rustic quality because it has been stamped in a muted green, then rubbed back to blend with the existing lettering on the wood. If you are lucky enough to find a custom-made wine crate like this one, it will simply need a good scrubbing with soapy water, then be left to dry before you stamp it.

You will need

- old wine crate or similar wooden box
- scrubbing brush (optional)
- emulsion (latex) paint in olive-green
- plate
- foam roller
- grape stamp
- fine abrasive paper (sandpaper)

1 If necessary, scrub the wine crate or box well with soapy water and a scrubbing brush. Leave the wood to dry.

2 Spread some olive-green paint on to a plate and run the roller through it until it is evenly coated. Ink the stamp and begin stamping a random pattern of grapes. Stamp at different angles to add variety.

3 Cover all the surfaces of the crate or box, overlapping the edge if the planks are too narrow to take the whole motif.

ABOVE: *Look out for a wooden crate or box with plenty of character. Your local wine merchant may be able to help.*

4 Leave the paint to dry, then rub back the pattern with abrasive paper (sandpaper) so that it becomes faded and blends with the original surface decoration or lettering. Rub gently and aim for a patchy, distressed appearance.

GILDED TRAY

This simple wooden tea tray is transformed into an item of historic grandeur by using an easy gilding technique. Begin by sanding away any old paint or varnish and painting the base of the tray in black and the sides in red-ochre emulsion (latex) paint, applying two or three coats. The heraldic motifs make up a central panel design, and the fine outline is repeated around the edge of the tray. The tray is stamped twice, first with the red-ochre paint and then with gold size, which is a transparent glue used for gilding. Dutch metal leaf is then applied over the size.

You will need

- wooden tea tray, prepared as above
- ruler
- pencil
- fleur-de-lys and diamond stamps
- black stamp pad
- scrap paper
- scissors
- emulsion (latex) paint in red-ochre
- plates
- foam roller
- thin wooden batten (furring strip)
- lining brush
- gold size and brush
- Dutch metal leaf
- soft and hard paintbrushes
- shellac and brush

1 Measure out and mark in pencil the six-sided central panel. Draw a border around the edge of the tray. Print eight fleurs-de-lys and five diamonds on to scrap paper and cut them out. Use them to plan your design, marking the base point of each motif in pencil on the tray. Spread some red-ochre paint on to a plate and run the roller through it until it is evenly coated. Ink the stamps and print the fleur-de-lys and diamond pattern.

2 Using the wooden batten (furring strip) to support your hand, use the lining brush and the red-ochre paint to paint a fine line around the design, following the pencil lines of the central panel. Paint another fine line just inside the edge of the tray. If you have never used a lining brush, practise making lines on scrap paper until you are confident with the technique.

3 Paint the sides of the tray with size. Leave the size to become tacky, according to the time specified by the manufacturer. Place one sheet of Dutch metal leaf on to the size at a time and burnish with the back of a soft brush. Spread the gold size on to a plate and use the roller to ink the stamps with size. Overprint the red-ochre patterns, stamping each print slightly down and to the left of the already printed motif to create a dropped shadow effect. Leave the size to become tacky and gild with Dutch metal leaf in the same way as before. Use a stiff paintbrush to sweep away the excess leaf. Seal the whole tray with a protective coat of shellac.

BELOW: This opulent treatment would also transform a plain wooden side table in a medieval-inspired drawing room.

TULIP TRAY

Paint and stamp a tray like this one and you will be tempted to display it rather than put it to practical use. You can in fact do both, if you apply several coats of varnish to give the tray a washable surface. The tulips and leaves are stamped on bold geometric shapes to give them added impact. The colours used here are not typical of folk art and give the tray a dramatic, contemporary look. You could use a more traditional colour combination, such as black, red and green, for a completely different effect.

You will need

- wooden tray
- emulsion (latex) paint in dusky blue, buttermilk-yellow and dark blue
- household paintbrushes
- ruler
- pencil
- plate
- foam roller
- tulip and leaf stamps
- clear satin varnish and brush

1 Paint the tray with dusky blue emulsion (latex) paint and leave to dry. Use a ruler and pencil to draw a square in the centre of the tray, then draw a square on the diagonal inside it. Add two rectangular panels on either side of the central square. The size of the panels will depend on the tray.

2 Paint the diagonal square and the two rectangles in buttermilk-yellow, and the remaining area of the larger square in dark blue. If your tray has cut-out handles, paint inside them in dark blue.

ABOVE: *Cheerful colours and bold shapes make a breakfast tray or television supper tray a pleasure to use. Choose a tray with high sides like this one.*

3 Spread some dark blue paint on to a plate and use the roller to ink the tulip and leaf stamps. Print two leaves on the side panels and two tulips in the central square, both end to end.

4 Apply at least three coats of clear satin varnish, allowing each coat to dry thoroughly before applying the next. The stamping will become more resistant with each coat of varnish.

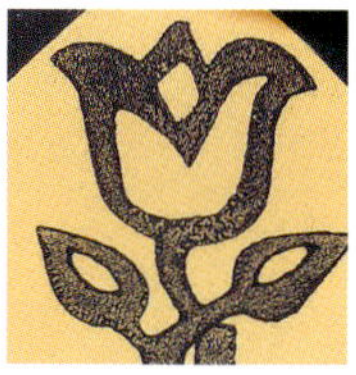

SEASIDE PICNIC

Picnics in cookbooks and magazine articles always look irresistibly inviting and miles away from the reality of hastily made sandwiches on an assortment of unbreakable plates. One of the problems about picnics is that they tend to be spontaneously arranged on a sunny day, so presentation gets forgotten. The trick is to prepare your picnic set ready for the next time the sun shines. For this project, you don't need to buy new picnic gear – old plates and napkins look perfect jumbled together when they are all stamped with the same design.

You will need

- wooden tray
- acrylic enamel paint in deep red and light blue
- plates
- foam rollers
- starfish, shell and seahorse stamps
- selection of plates and platters
- scrap paper
- scissors
- pencil
- checked napkins and tablecloth
- backing paper
- fabric paint in sea-green
- iron

1 To stamp the tray, spread some of the deep red paint on to a plate and run a roller through it until it is evenly coated. Ink the starfish stamp with the roller and make the first print in a corner of the tray.

2 Print a starfish in the other three corners, then ink the shell stamp and make one print in the centre of the tray. Print seahorses all along the outside edges of the tray.

3 To stamp the plates, ink the seahorse stamp with deep red paint and print on to a piece of scrap paper. Cut out the motif and plan your design by positioning the seahorse round each plate and marking with a pencil where each stamp will go.

4 Ink the stamp and print the first seahorse, following your pencil marks as a guide for positioning.

5 Re-ink the stamp and turn it the other way round for the next print. Continue turning the stamp each time you print so that heads meet heads and tails meet tails.

6 To stamp the platters, spread some light blue paint on to a plate and run a roller through it until it is evenly coated. Ink the starfish stamp and print in two opposite corners of each platter.

7 Ink the shell stamp with the light blue paint and make a print next to one of the starfish.

8 Print one more shell motif as shown, then complete the platter design by adding two seahorse motifs in the remaining spaces.

9 Protect your work surface with backing paper and lay a napkin over this. Count the checks to decide on the spacing of your design. Spread some sea-green fabric paint on to a plate and run a roller through it until it is evenly coated. Ink the shell stamp and make the first print in one corner.

10 Stamp a shell in each corner of the napkin, then ink the seahorse stamp and make a print by the side of each shell.

11 Ink the starfish stamp and complete the border pattern by printing a starfish in the remaining spaces on the border. Stamp the tablecloth to match the napkins. Fix (set) the fabric paint with a hot iron, following the manufacturer's instructions.

RIGHT: It is easy to make this co-ordinated picnic set. Stamping on to checked fabric gives even simple motifs extra interest. It also provides a grid which makes positioning the stamps very straightforward. Now all you need is the food!

CHILDREN'S ROOMS

Children grow up and change their ideas very quickly, so decorating on their behalf presents its own particular problems. Realistically you must expect them to demand a completely new decor around every five years. This can be quite liberating, however, as you don't have to think in the very long term, so throw caution to the wind and enjoy yourself. While the decor of their room might be important to some children, most – especially younger ones – will be happy for you to make the decorating decisions for them. Whether you are decorating for a baby, a young child or a young adult, these rooms should inspire you to be creative and individual.

ABOVE: Decorate whole walls or individual pieces of furniture to give your child's room a truly individual look.

LEFT: As well as ready-made stamps, simple sponge shapes are ideal. You can even use pre-cut children's bath sponges.

NURSERY WALLS

Children are often bombarded with a riot of primary colours or surrounded in pretty pastels, so this dark colour scheme provides an unusual and refreshing change. It gives the room a wonderful period feel and the deep blue-green shade is known for its calming effect. You can offset the dark colour by painting a light colour above the dado (chair) rail and laying a lighter, natural floor covering like sisal or cork tiles. The effect is rich and intense. This idea can be adapted to any colour scheme and you can reverse the effect by using a light background with darker stamps. Experiment with colours and shades and you'll often find that unusual combinations create the most stunning impact.

You will need

- emulsion (latex) paint in deep blue-green, sap-green and red
- household paintbrush
- plates
- foam roller
- large heart stamp
- water-based matt (flat) varnish and brush (optional)

1 Paint the wall below the dado (chair) rail in deep blue-green. Leave to dry. Spread a small amount of sap-green paint on to a plate and run the roller through it until it is evenly coated. Ink the stamp and begin printing the pattern in groups. Re-ink the stamp only when the print is very light.

2 Gradually build up the pattern all over the wall. The first prints after inking will be solid and bright; the last ones will fade into the background. This is a feature of the design, so make the most of the natural irregularities.

3 This is an optional step. If you find that the contrasts are too strong, mix some varnish with the blue-green paint (one part paint to five parts varnish) and brush it all over the pattern. Leave to dry.

4 Ink the stamp with red paint and overprint every third heart in the top row. Then overprint every third heart in the next row, this time starting one in from the edge. Repeat these two rows to overprint the whole pattern. Only re-ink the stamp when the colour has faded.

BELOW: A single repeated motif will look varied and interesting if you only re-ink the stamp occasionally.

POLKA-DOT BEDROOM WALLS

Deciding on the bedroom decor for older children can sometimes be difficult. They are definitely not babies and probably don't want a themed room. However, something light-hearted and not too fussy can be hard to achieve. A spot is the simplest of motifs and can be used on its own or in combination with other shapes. Stars can be added as a variation, or darker spots stamped below the dado (chair) rail. The end result is far from childish but neither is it too sombre. The colours used here are quite sophisticated but another combination would change the mood completely.

You will need

- pair of compasses
- scrap paper
- scissors
- low-density sponge, such as a bath sponge
- felt-tipped pen
- craft knife
- emulsion (latex) paint in dusky blue
- plate
- plumbline (optional)
- ruler (optional)
- emulsion paint in black and yellow (optional)

1 Use a pair of compasses to draw a circle with a diameter of 8cm/$3\frac{1}{4}$in on scrap paper. Cut it out.

2 Using this circle as a template, draw two circles on the sponge with a felt-tipped pen.

3 Cut out the circles with a craft knife. First cut around the outline, then part the sponge and cut right through to the other side.

4 If you are using star motifs as well as the spots, draw out a star shape on another piece of sponge and cut it out with a craft knife.

5 Spread an even coating of dusky blue paint on to a plate and press the spot stamp into it. Make a test print on to scrap paper to ensure that the stamp is not overloaded. If you trust your eye, then begin printing the spots in evenly spaced rows. If you need a guide, attach a plumbline at ceiling height and stamp the spots alongside it, measuring the distance between the spots with a ruler. Move the line along a measured distance and repeat the process.

6 For a more dramatic effect, darken the blue down a tone by adding some black, then stamp more spot motifs below the dado (chair) rail.

7 If you are using the star motif too, dip the sponge into yellow paint, test on scrap paper, and stamp stars at equal intervals between the spots. For further interest, you could mix a darker yellow, and stamp over the original stars, slightly off-centre, to create a dropped shadow effect.

RIGHT: Position the sponge stamps by eye or, if you are nervous about this, use a plumbline and a ruler to mark out an evenly spaced pattern.

CARIBBEAN BATHROOM

Bathtime should be a fun-filled part of a child's day but sometimes there is a certain reluctance to enter the bathroom. Encourage your child by decorating the walls with bright and cheerful motifs. This bathroom has a tropical seaside theme. The intense sky-blue of the background is separated from the sandy yellow by a bright red peg rail, a feature that is both decorative and extremely functional. The stamps are pre-cut bath sponges. We have copied the sponge colours here, but you could choose any colour combination you wished.

You will need

- emulsion (latex) paint in viridian-green, pink and yellow
- plates
- scrap paper
- set of tropical-theme sponges

1 Spread even coatings of veridian-green, pink and yellow paint on to separate plates. Press the palm tree sponge into the green, then make a test print on scrap paper to ensure that the sponge is not overloaded with paint. Stamp the first print at a 45-degree angle, just above the peg rail.

2 Press the fish sponge into the pink paint and make a test print on scrap paper. Then stamp the fish beside the palm tree. Once again avoid an upright print, angle it slightly.

3 Press the pineapple sponge into the yellow paint, make a test print on paper, then stamp it above the others, once again at a 45-degree angle.

4 Continue stamping the three shapes until they fill the wall. Position the prints close to one another, and change the angle of the print each time so that the pattern is densely packed and completely random.

BELOW: This design uses pre-cut children's bath sponges. Many other shapes are readily available to buy.

APPLE TREE MURAL

It is advisable to undertake this project when the children are out of the way. This sort of decorating is very appealing to young people and they will want to join in. However, if you are willing to let them help you, be prepared for a less stylish and more spontaneous result. The apple tree mural is perfect for a playroom or for a new baby's room. It is the kind of design that will last throughout childhood, as it will not appear babyish too quickly. The mural was painted with pieces of sponge instead of a brush to harmonize all the textures, so that the tree, leaves and fruit all have the same soft finish. The colours are muted to prevent the design becoming too overbearing.

You will need

- stiff card (stock)
- pencil
- craft knife
- felt-tipped pen
- low-density sponge, such as a bath sponge
- diluted emulsion (latex) paint in pink, brick-red, yellow, sap-green, blue-grey, ochre and olive-green
- plates
- paintbrush
- scrap paper

1 Draw the branch, trunk and base shapes on to a sheet of stiff card (stock). Carefully cut out the shapes with a craft knife.

2 Using a felt-tipped pen, draw a circle and a leaf on to the sponge. Cut around the outline, then part the sponge and cut right through.

3 Decide where to position the trees on the wall, then draw around the base template in pencil.

4 Draw the tree trunk above the base, using a long, rectangular shape as a template.

5 Add six curved branches. Stagger three branches up one side of the tree trunk, then flip the template over to draw three matching branches opposite them.

6 Spread the paints out on to separate plates using a paintbrush. For the tree's base you will need pink, brick-red, yellow and sap-green. Starting at the skirting (base) board, use a piece of sponge to fill in the pencil outline drawn on the wall. Make a test print on scrap paper first to ensure that the sponge is not overloaded.

7 Fill in the tree trunk and the branches with the blue-grey paint. The sponging should not look perfect; it should be textured and rough. Cut the sponge into a point at one end to print the ends of the branches.

8 Stamp the leaves in ochre and olive-green. Over-stamp one colour with the other occasionally, to give a three-dimensional effect.

9 Finally, use the sponge circle and pink paint to stamp the apples. Space them randomly in the foliage. Print some apples to overlap the leaves and print others partially, as if obscured by the leaves. Apply more pressure to one side of the sponge; it will print darker and give the fruit a shaded effect.

RIGHT: A mixture of sponge painting and stamping gives this beautiful mural a lovely delicate appearance.

"COUNTRY QUILT" FRIEZE

Stamp this friendly, folk-style frieze in a child's bedroom in soft pinks and a warm green. The pattern is reminiscent of an old-fashioned American appliqué quilt. The overlapping edges and jauntily angled birds accentuate its naive charm. The colour scheme avoids the harshness of primaries which are so often chosen for children. Green is a calming colour but it can be cold. For this project use a sap-green, which contains a lot of yellow, for warmth. The finished effect is bright enough to be eye-catching without being overpowering.

You will need

- emulsion (latex) or artist's acrylic paint in sap-green, pink and crimson
- household paintbrush
- pencil
- ruler
- spirit level
- medium-density sponge, such as a kitchen sponge
- craft knife
- tracing paper
- spray adhesive
- plates

1 Divide the wall by painting the lower section sap-green, up to dado (chair) rail height. Measure 24cm/9½in up from the green section and draw a straight line using a pencil, ruler and spirit level to act as a guide for the top of the border. Cut a straight strip of foam, 2cm/¾in wide, using a craft knife.

2 Trace and transfer all the pattern shapes from the template section, then spray with adhesive. Stick them on to the foam and cut out with a craft knife. Press the straight strip into the green paint and make a test print. Print a line along the pencil guideline, then another just above the green wall section.

3 Press the curved strip into the green paint, make a test print, then stamp curved lines to form a branch.

4 Press the leaf shape into the green paint, make a test print, then stamp the leaves in groups, as shown, two above and one below the branch.

5 Stamp pale pink birds along the branch – you need two prints, one facing each direction. Do not make the prints too uniform; aim for a patchy, textured effect.

6 Clean the bird stamp, then press it into the crimson paint. Stamp the rest of the birds along the branch, alternating the direction of the motif as before.

7 Stamp a row of pink and crimson hearts above the top line to complete the frieze pattern.

HEARTS TOY BOX

This project gives instant appeal to the most ordinary of wooden boxes. It works just as well on old as new woods, but if you are using an old box give it a good rub down with medium- and fine-grade abrasive paper (sandpaper) before you begin. This will remove any sharp edges or splinters. The box is given a rust-red background before being stamped with three different heart shapes in four colours. The stamps are rotated so that they appear at different angles and the pattern turns out quite randomly. It is best to follow the spirit of the idea rather than adhering rigidly to the instructions. That way, you will end up with a truly individual design.

You will need

- hinged wooden chest/box with a lid (suitable for storing toys)
- emulsion (latex) paint in rust-red
- household paintbrush
- emulsion or acrylic paint in maroon, sap-green, bright green and dark blue
- plates
- foam rollers
- small, large and trellis heart stamps
- fine-grade abrasive paper (sandpaper)
- matt (flat) varnish and brush

1 Paint the box with rust-red paint, applying two coats to give a good matt background. Leave the paint to dry between coats.

2 Spread some maroon paint on to a plate and run a roller through it until it is evenly coated. Use the roller to apply a border round the edge of the lid. Leave to dry.

3 Spread some sap-green paint on to a plate and coat a roller. Ink the small heart stamp and print a few hearts randomly over the lid of the box.

4 Ink the large and the trellis heart stamps with the sap-green paint. Print some hearts close together and others on their own to create a random pattern. Cover the whole box in this way.

5 Clean all three stamps and ink with the bright green paint. Build up the pattern by adding this colour in the gaps, leaving enough space for the last two colours.

6 Clean the stamps. Using the dark blue paint, continue stamping the three hearts over the box.

7 Clean the stamps. Finally, fill in the remaining background space with the maroon paint and the three heart stamps. No large spaces should remain. Leave to dry completely.

8 Use fine-grade abrasive paper (sandpaper) to rub down the box where you think natural wear and tear would be most likely to occur.

9 You can preserve the comfortable "weathered" look of the toy box by applying two coats of matt (flat) varnish. Leave to dry between coats.

RIGHT: Unusual colours give this design real impact. If you prefer, you can stamp the hearts in primary or pastel colours to fit in with the rest of the room. Paint the box in a background colour that will show off the motifs.

MINIBUS TOY BOX

Every child should be encouraged to tidy away his or her toys at the end of the day. This eye-catching toy box might just do the trick! The pastel-coloured patches behind the bus stamps give the box a 1950s look. These patches are stencilled on to a light turquoise background. Stamp the buses on quite randomly so that some extend beyond the patch shapes. Keep changing the angle of the stamp – the effect will be almost three-dimensional.

You will need

- hinged wooden box
- emulsion (latex) paint in light turquoise
- household paintbrush
- pencil
- ruler
- sheet of stencil card (stock) or mylar
- spray adhesive
- craft knife
- emulsion or stencil paint in yellow, pink and pastel blue
- plates
- small paint roller
- stamping ink in brown
- minibus rubber stamp
- rubber roller

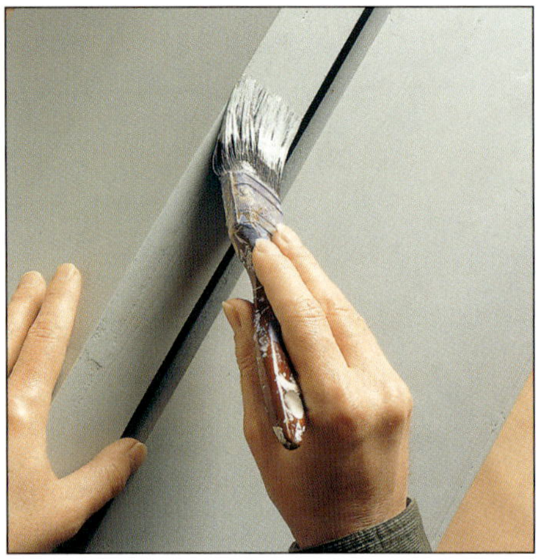

1 Apply two coats of light turquoise emulsion (latex) paint to the box. Leave to dry. Draw and cut out a stencil for the background shape. It should be large enough to contain the whole stamp image plus a small border.

2 Spread the yellow, pink and pastel blue paints on to separate plates. Using a small paint roller, paint the first colour through the stencil on to the box. You will need an equal number of shapes for each colour.

3 Wash the roller and apply the two remaining colours, painting through the stencil as before. Balance the shapes with an equal amount of background colour. Leave to dry.

4 Pour some brown stamping ink on to a clean plate. Coat the rubber stamp with ink using a rubber roller.

5 Stamp the bus motifs on to the pastel patches. Allow the stamps to overlap some of the patches and vary the angle of the stamp.

ABOVE: Use a stamp that will reflect your child's interests and hobbies. There is a wide selection of ready-made stamps to choose from. Position the stamps at jaunty angles, with some overlapping the box lid.

TEMPLATES

The templates on the following pages may be resized to any scale required. The simplest way of doing this is to enlarge them on a photocopier, or trace the design and draw a grid of evenly spaced squares over your tracing. Draw a larger grid on another piece of paper and copy the outline square by square. Draw over the lines to make sure they are continuous.

SPINNING SUN MOTIF
page 32

FLORAL SPRIG
page 30

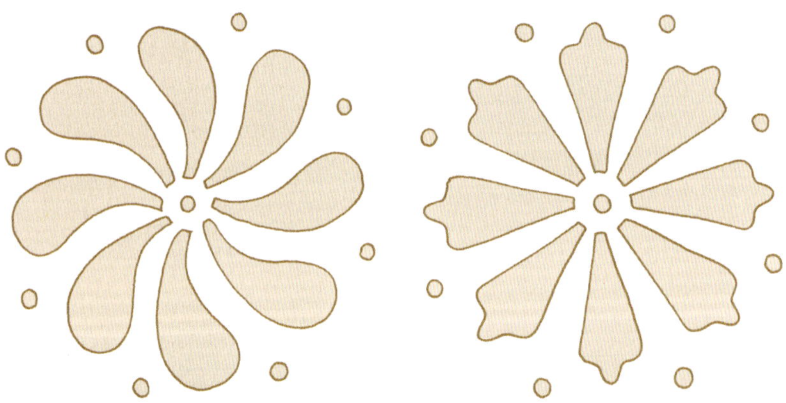

SCANDINAVIAN LIVING ROOM
page 40

MEXICAN BORDER
page 37

SUNSTAR WALL
page 34

STAR CABINET
page 96

GREEK KEY
BATHROOM
page 76

SPRIGGED CALICO
CURTAINS
page 124

FISH FOOTSTOOL
page 88

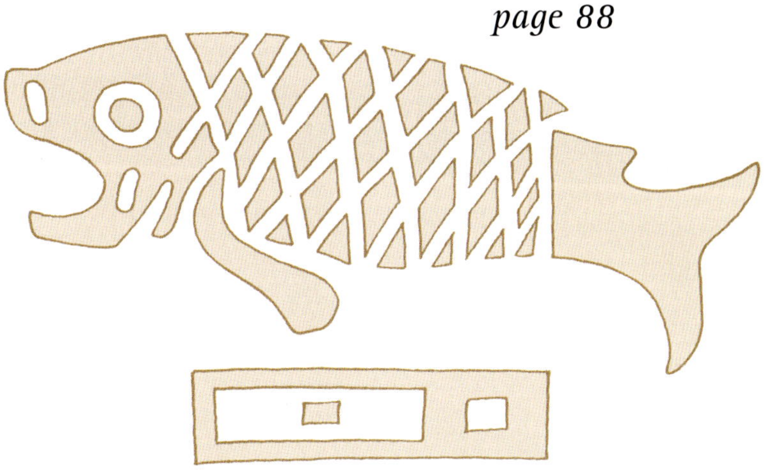

FOLK MOTIF CHAIR
page 90

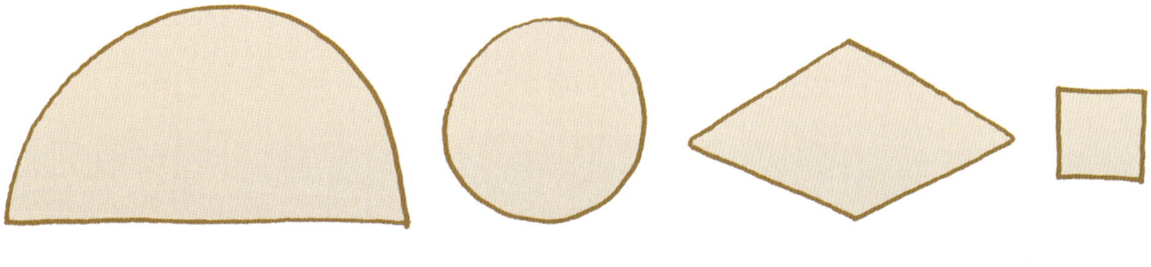

NO-SEW STAR CURTAIN
page 122

PERSONALIZED FLOWERPOTS
page 148

SNOWFLAKE STORAGE JARS
page 168

SEEDPOD
LAMPSHADE
page 206

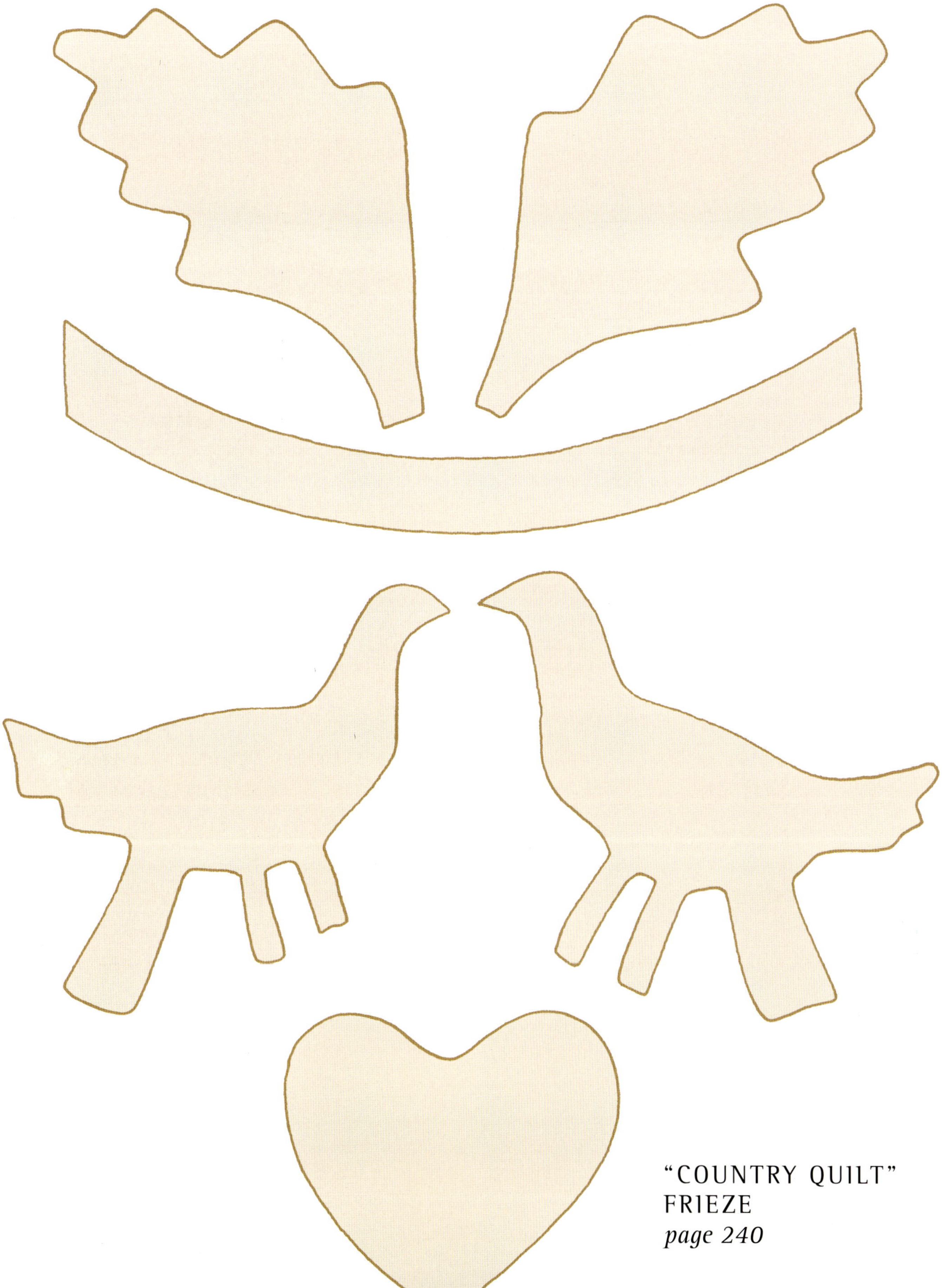

"COUNTRY QUILT"
FRIEZE
page 240

INDEX

G

H

I

J

K

L

M

N

G

H

I

J

K

L

M

N